Remarkable Children

Twenty
Who
Made
History

**by
Dennis
Brindell
Fradin**

Little, Brown and Company
Boston   Toronto

For my father,
Myron Fradin

First Edition

The author is grateful to the following for permission to reprint excerpts from previously copyrighted material:

The poems of Hilda Conkling are reprinted by permission of Mrs.
Elsa Kruuse, Executrix of the Estate of Hilda Conkling, and first appeared in *Poems by a Little Girl* (1920) and *Shoes of the Wind* (1922), both
published by Frederick A. Stokes.

Excerpts from *Anne Frank: The Diary of a Young Girl* by Anne Frank
are reprinted by permission of Doubleday & Company, Inc., and Val-
lentine, Mitchell & Co., Ltd. Copyright 1952 by Otto H. Frank.

Library of Congress Cataloging-in-Publication Data
Fradin, Dennis B.
    Remarkable children.

    Summary: Presents brief biographies of twenty children from dif-
ferent places and times who gained fame in childhood for their unusual
talents and remarkable achievements.
    1. Children — Biography — Juvenile literature.
    2. World history — Juvenile literature. [1. Children —
Biography] I. Title.
CT107.F65 1987   920'.02 [920]   87-3820
ISBN 0-316-29126-9 (lib. bdg.)

Designed by Trisha Hanlon

RRD — VA

Published simultaneously in Canada
by Little, Brown & Company (Canada) Limited

Printed in the United States of America

Contents

Preface   v

Wolfgang Amadeus Mozart (1756–1791)   3
  A famous musician at the age of six

John Quincy Adams (1767–1848)   13
  A fourteen-year-old diplomatic secretary

Sacagawea (1789?–1812?)   23
  *Interpreter for the Lewis and Clark Expedition
  at sixteen*

Mary Anning (1799–1847)   36
  Discoverer of a fossil skeleton at eleven

Zerah Colburn (1804–1839)   43
  A seven-year-old mathematical prodigy

Louis Braille (1809–1852)   55
  *Inventor of the braille reading system
  for the blind at fifteen*

María de Sautuola (1870–1946)   65
  *An eight-year-old discoverer of prehistoric
  cave paintings*

Helen Keller (1880–1968)   73
  *Surmounter of major physical handicaps
  by the age of ten*

Pablo Picasso (1881–1973)   86
  An award-winning artist by the age of fifteen
Hilda Conkling (1910–1986)   94
  A published poet at nine
Judy Garland (1922–1969)   103
  Star of radio, vaudeville, and the movies
  by the age of fourteen
Shirley Temple (born in 1928)   115
  The world's most popular movie star
  at the age of seven
Anne Frank (1929–1945)   124
  Thirteen-year-old author of a famous wartime diary
Muhammad Adh-Dhîb (born in 1931 or 1932) 137
  Fifteen-year-old discoverer of
  the Dead Sea Scrolls
Pelé (born in 1940)   146
  A professional soccer player at fifteen
Muhammad Ali (born Cassius Clay
  in 1942)   156
  A boxer on television at thirteen
Bobby Fischer (born in 1943)   166
  Chess champion of the United States at fourteen
Mark Whitaker (born in 1951)   176
  A sixteen-year-old discoverer of a comet
Nadia Comaneci (born in 1961)   185
  Olympic gold medal winner at fourteen
Tracy Austin (born in 1962)   197
  Winner of the U.S. women's tennis
  championship at sixteen

Preface

One day when I had finished all my other writing projects, I opened my IDEAS folder for inspiration. Three notes among the dozens I had put in there over the years seemed to have special potential. One was about Zerah Colburn, a seven-year-old Vermont math whiz who could figure out the number of seconds in two thousand years faster than you could say his name. The second note was about María de Sautuola, eight-year-old discoverer of the prehistoric artwork in Spain's Altamira Cave. On the third I had jotted something about Mary Anning, the eleven-year-old English girl who discovered the first complete skeleton of the enormous reptile Ichthyosaurus.

As I stood there with that messy folder in my hands, a light bulb switched on inside my brain's dusty caverns. Why not write a book about a number of remarkable child achievers?

Only one thing worried me as I began my planning. What if I had trouble finding children outside sports, music, and entertainment — fields in which young people have traditionally done well? After a little research, I was happy to learn that children have excelled in many of the same fields as adults. They have written books and made scientific discoveries, created outstanding paintings, and even participated in politics.

I also wondered if the children I was writing about shared some quality that helped them succeed. This didn't turn out to be the case, either. Instead, I learned that children have done remarkable things for the same variety of reasons one can find among adult achievers. Some, such as Mozart and Pablo Picasso, were geniuses. Others, such as chess champion Bobby Fischer, had remarkable determination. A number of them were groomed for greatness — or even shoved into it — by their parents. And a few, such as María de Sautuola, were just plain lucky.

Their youth did tend to make my remarkable children unique in several ways, though. Often they had to deal with success, fame, fortune, and responsibility just a few years after they stopped wearing diapers. And if their fame passed, they had to cope with being "over the hill" at an age when everyone else was planning for future success.

I learned about these remarkable children by reading about them, and in several cases also by talking to them and to those who knew them. In the process, I have come to feel that all of these remarkable children are personal friends. I hope that when you finish this book you'll feel the same way.

D.B.F.

Remarkable Children

Wolfgang Amadeus Mozart

(1756–1791)

One night in the year 1760, in a fourth-floor apartment in Salzburg, Austria, Wolfgang Mozart was sitting at the clavier making marks on paper when his father and a family friend entered the room. "What are you doing?" asked Leopold Mozart, who was a well-known music teacher and composer in Salzburg.

"Writing a concerto for the clavier," answered the four-year-old boy. "The first part is almost done."

Herr Mozart and the family friend, a trumpeter named Andreas Schachtner, exchanged smiles, for how could a four-year-old compose a concerto?

"It must be something very fine. Let me see," said Herr Mozart, picking up the piece.

As the two men studied his composition, Wolfgang saw the smiles leave their faces. With wonder and delight in his eyes, Wolfgang's father said, "Look how correct and orderly it is, Herr Schachtner. Only it is so very difficult that nobody could play it." Andreas Schachtner, who described this scene in detail in a letter he wrote more than thirty years later, related that Wolfgang further amazed the two adults by playing the complex piece he had just composed.

When this occurred, Wolfgang had been surprising people with his musical ability for more than a year. As soon as they had been able to sit up, Wolfgang and his sister, Nannerl, had been taught by their father to play the clavier, a keyboard instrument similar to the piano. Nannerl, who was four and a half years older than Wolfgang, had shown talent at this instrument. Wolfgang had so amazed people by his ability that some had proclaimed him a *Wunderkind* — a wonder child. From time to time there had been other musical *Wunderkinder* who had stunned people with their ability to play the violin or some other instrument. But the creation of an intricate musical composition at the age of four was something that placed Wolfgang in a class by himself.

Convinced that Wolfgang was destined to become one of the great musical geniuses of all time, Leopold Mozart saved the boy's early compositions and began taking notes on his musical progress. Because of his effort, we have a fine record of Wolfgang Amadeus Mozart's musical development.

Music was crucial to every aspect of Wolfgang's life. When he wasn't practicing, taking a clavier or violin lesson from his father, or composing music of his own, Wolfgang liked to copy pieces written by the great composers of the past. When he and Nannerl played together, they gave their games a musical accompaniment by singing duets, and when they were called to the dinner table, they composed march tunes while walking out of the room. Wolfgang even had a musical bedtime ritual. Every night his father had to pick him up, carry him into his bedroom, and sit him down in a chair. Then Wolfgang and his father would sing the special bedtime song made of meaningless words that the boy had composed:

Oragna figata fà, marina gamina fà.

Then Wolfgang would climb into bed, probably to think about grace notes, minor scales, and arpeggios until he fell asleep!

When he was five years old, Wolfgang began playing with Nannerl at recitals arranged by their father. Wolfgang enjoyed the attention, applause, and adoration he received from the people of Salzburg, but he was a high-strung child who would burst into tears or even stop playing if someone spoke or left the room while he was performing. Another aspect of his sensitivity was his delicate ear. Certain sounds caused him pain. Andreas Schachtner later wrote that Wolfgang was even upset by certain instruments:

> Almost up to his tenth year he had an insurmountable dread of the trumpet when it was played alone without other instruments; if one merely held out a trumpet towards him it was as if one had pointed a loaded pistol at his heart. His father wanted to rid him of this childish fear and asked me once in spite of his objections to blow towards him, but, my God! I had to desist. Wolfgang no sooner heard the clanging sound than he turned pale, began to totter and would have fallen into convulsions had I not stopped.

When Wolfgang was still only five, his parents (probably mainly his father, who dominated his life) decided that it would be better for him to study music at home than to take a general course of studies at school like other children. Herr Mozart organized Wolfgang's day into separate periods, just like those the boy would have experienced at school.

There were periods for clavier and violin practice, a period for singing lessons, and a time for composing. Wolfgang didn't think of his rigid schedule as work, because music gave him so much pleasure. When his lessons were done, he would continue to practice on his own. In fact, Wolfgang's parents had trouble getting him to leave his music to eat a meal or play outside with other children.

By the time Wolfgang was six, Leopold Mozart decided that the boy was ready to display his genius to the world. In those days kings, queens, and other rulers governed various parts of Europe. Dreaming that his children would make a fortune by playing before these important persons, Leopold Mozart began to map out trips to various palaces.

The family's first trip was to the court at Munich, Germany, early in 1762. Wolfgang and Nannerl played before the nobles at the palace, where they were greatly admired and showered with gold and silver coins.

Leopold Mozart was so encouraged by this first success that he planned a trip to Vienna, where Empress Maria Theresa ruled over the countries now known as Austria, Hungary, and part of Czechoslovakia. Wolfgang's father thought of a way to make money as they stopped at various cities on the way to Vienna. At each stop Leopold would obtain permission for Wolfgang to play the organ at the biggest church in town. As the *Wunderkind* played, people would flock to the church to hear the free recital. Later, when Wolfgang gave a concert where admission was charged, many of these same people would pay to hear him again.

After several weeks on the road, the Mozart family arrived in Vienna, where Wolfgang and Nannerl gave several preliminary performances to admiring nobles. Then on the morning of October 13, 1762, Frau Mozart dressed Wolfgang and Nannerl in their finest clothes and polished all their buttons. That afternoon the empress's carriage arrived at the hotel to pick up all the Mozarts except Mother, who had decided to wait in their hotel room.

The two children and their father were helped into the carriage by footmen in braided uniforms, and a few minutes later they arrived at the magnificent palace. Apparently Wolfgang wasn't overwhelmed by all the gold, crystal, and silk that met his eyes, for when he was brought before the empress he suddenly jumped onto her lap, placed his arms around her neck, and gave her a big kiss. Although his father was taken aback by this, Maria Theresa fortunately wasn't. The empress, who had borne sixteen children herself, enjoyed the young genius's show of affection.

Wolfgang, Nannerl, and their father were soon led into the music room. For the next several hours the two children played the clavier and the harpsichord while the empress, emperor, and their children listened. After the concert, the royal children took Wolfgang and Nannerl on a tour of the palace. They were in the midst of the tour when Wolfgang suddenly slipped and fell on a highly polished floor. Princess Marie Antoinette, who was almost exactly the same age as Wolfgang, held out her hands and pulled him back to his feet.

"When I grow up, I am going to marry you!" Wolfgang told Marie Antoinette, who later became the queen of France.

After their highly successful performance at the palace, Wolfgang and Nannerl played before other aristocrats in Vienna. Soon the two children were the rage of the city. Money, clothes, and presents were showered upon them, and they received more invitations to play than they could possibly fulfill. Unfortunately, Wolfgang, who wasn't getting the proper sleep or fresh air, was stricken with a serious fever. It took the thin, frail boy several weeks to recover from his illness.

Thanks to newspaper stories and word of mouth, the Mozarts were in great demand throughout Europe by the time they returned to Salzburg. For the next several years Leopold Mozart took his children to palaces, concert halls, and homes throughout the continent. The two children — and especially Wolfgang — were a great sensation in Frankfurt, Cologne, Brussels, Paris, The Hague, and London. A highlight of their London trip was

Wolfgang and Nannerl's performance for King George III and Queen Charlotte.

Wherever Wolfgang and Nannerl played, Herr Mozart wrote what would now be called "press releases" and sent them to the local newspapers. Here is one, written by Leopold Mozart more than two centuries ago:

> The little girl, who is in her twelfth year, will play the most difficult compositions of the greatest masters; the boy, who is not yet seven, . . . will also play a concerto for the violin, and will accompany symphonies on the clavier, the manual or keyboard being covered with a cloth, with as much facility as if he could see the keys; he will instantly name all notes played at a distance, whether singly or in chords, on the clavier, or any other instrument, glass, bell, or clock. He will finally, both on the harpsichord and the organ, improvise as long as may be desired and in any key, thus proving that he is as thoroughly acquainted with the one instrument as with the other, great as is the difference between them.
>
> Each person pays half-a-thaler. Tickets may be had at the Golden Lion.

By the time Wolfgang was seven years old, he was being hailed as one of the greatest child performers of all time and was also known as a fine composer. At just five years of age, Wolfgang had composed a minuet that is still performed today. In 1763, when he was seven, Wolfgang's first compositions were published. By the time he was twelve he was regularly being commissioned by wealthy people to compose operas, symphonies, sonatas, and masses.

Because of his hope that his children would make the family wealthy, Leopold Mozart neglected his own career and continued to travel with Nannerl and Wolfgang. It turned out, however, that the children didn't make nearly as much money as he had expected. Instead of money, they were often presented with snuffboxes, watches, ribbons, and awards. Despite their great fame, Nannerl and Wolfgang had to perform continually just to do a little bit better than pay for the family's traveling expenses.

When Wolfgang reached his teens, he began to resent several aspects of his performing schedule. For one thing, he was tired of doing what he called "circus stunts," such as playing with the keyboard covered. He also was starting to resent the way his father continually pushed and promoted him in an attempt to make money. By Wolfgang's sixteenth birthday, even Leopold could see that they weren't going to earn the fortune he had dreamed about. Nannerl had long since stopped performing with Wolfgang. As for the *Wunderkind,* Wolfgang was acknowledged as a genius by critics and music lovers. To the general public, however, the teen-aged Wolfgang was no longer a novelty. Most of those who had thrown gold to him when he'd been a child had no interest in him as an adult.

Wolfgang's troubles intensified throughout his short life. Relations between Wolfgang and his father worsened, especially when Leopold opposed Wolf-gang's marriage to a young woman from Mann-heim, Germany. Wolfgang, his wife, and their two children lived a life of poverty. He earned money by composing, performing at recitals, and giving music lessons, but it never amounted to much. Con-tinual financial worries and the fact that he had worn out his body performing night and day in his early years contributed to Mozart's early death at the age of thirty-five.

Although he died in poverty, Mozart had left behind a wealth of beautiful music. Among his compositions are the operas *The Marriage of Figaro, Don Giovanni,* and *The Magic Flute;* the Requiem and other church music; the *Jupiter* Symphony and many other symphonies; and numerous pieces for piano and violin. These wonderful works have earned him a reputation as one of the greatest composers who ever lived.

John Quincy Adams

(1767–1848)

Many people know that John Quincy Adams was the sixth President of the United States and that he was the son of John Adams, the second President. Few know, however, that John Quincy Adams helped his country in several vital ways before he was fifteen years old.

From 1774 through 1776 John Quincy's father, John Adams, was frequently away from home. He was in Philadelphia serving in the Continental Congress, the convention that was then in the process of forming a new country — the United States of America. Because Mr. Adams was spending little time at his home in Braintree (now Quincy), Massachusetts, he communicated with his family through letters. From the letters his wife, Abigail, sent him, he learned about the progress and growth of their children. In return, he informed his family about the news coming out of Philadelphia. For example, in the summer of 1776 he wrote to his family about the important document he was ready to sign — the Declaration of Independence.

There was so much news in 1776 that Abigail Adams didn't want to wait for the sporadic mail deliveries. One day she asked nine-year-old John if he could fetch the family mail from Boston, about ten miles from their home. Thereafter, every few days Johnny rode to the Massachusetts capital to get the mail. Before his return trip he would stop for some refreshment at a Boston inn. There he would listen to the adults talk about the Revolution, which was then going very poorly for the Americans. In fact, in 1776 and 1777 it looked quite likely that the British would squash the American rebellion.

Late in 1777 the Continental Congress decided to send John Adams to Paris to help Benjamin Franklin obtain the help of the French for the American cause. While John Adams was home getting his affairs in order for the trip, he mentioned to Mrs. Adams that perhaps Johnny could go with him on the voyage. Johnny was an extremely studious and serious boy, who loved to awaken at dawn and study Latin or read a few pages of Tobias Smollett's *Complete History of England*. Abigail Adams agreed that a trip to France would be very educational for their oldest son. When John Adams asked Johnny to accompany him on this important trip, the boy gladly agreed.

Johnny and his father packed their bags, and on a February morning in 1778 they went by carriage from their farm to the port city of Marblehead, twenty miles northeast of Boston. They boarded the frigate *Boston,* and three days later they set sail for Bordeaux, France, more than thirty-five hundred miles away.

In those days, an Atlantic crossing was hazardous even in ordinary times. What made this trip especially dangerous was the fact that the British were eager to capture Johnny's father, who was one of the leading American patriots. If John Adams were captured, he would certainly be either jailed or hanged.

When the *Boston* was several days out of Marblehead, it was approached by three British men-o'-war. Johnny and his father raced to their cabin, where they packed all of Mr. Adams's papers into a weighted sack. They were prepared to throw the sack overboard in case the British seized their ship, but, thanks to favorable winds, the *Boston* managed to slip away.

Soon after that, the *Boston*'s lookout spotted

another British ship, the *Martha*. The captain explained to Mr. Adams that it would be safer to outrun the ship than to engage her in battle, but Mr. Adams insisted that they try to capture the *Martha* instead of fleeing.

Although the captain asked that they return to their cabin, John Adams got out his musket and went out onto the deck with Johnny. This could have resulted in the deaths of two future presidents of the United States, because at one point in the battle with the *Martha* a cannonball passed very close to John and John Quincy Adams before smashing into their ship. After a tremendous fight, the American ship finally prevailed. The captain of the *Boston* then dispatched several of his men to take the *Martha* back to the United States as a prize of war.

The rest of the voyage was relatively uneventful. To prepare for living in Paris, Johnny spent much of his time during the ocean crossing studying French. By the time they reached the coast of France, he knew the language quite well.

Once they arrived in Paris, Johnny and his father took lodgings in the same hotel that Benjamin Franklin, who had been trying to gain the support of the French for nearly a year, lived in. While his father spent his days working with Franklin, Johnny attended school at a boarding academy. All week he studied French, Latin, dancing, fencing, art, and music. Then on Friday afternoon his father would pick him up in a carriage, and the two of them would spend the weekend entertaining themselves at theaters, museums, gardens, and the Paris zoo, occasionally accompanied by Benjamin Franklin.

Thanks mainly to the work of the seventy-two-year-old Franklin, the French promised to provide soldiers, weapons, and money to the Americans. When John Adams had done all he could to help Franklin negotiate with the French, he and Johnny headed for home. Before they sailed, they stopped in the city of Nantes, France, to visit an American merchant named Joshua Johnson. Mr. Johnson had a daughter named Louisa Catherine, whom Johnny barely noticed because she was only four years old. Eighteen years later John Quincy was to marry Louisa Catherine Johnson.

Johnny and his father sailed from France in the spring of 1779, and on a morning in early August of that year they arrived at the Adams farm. After a year and a half away from home, Johnny was thrilled to be reunited with his mother, his sisters, and his brothers. The twelve-year-old was happy to be home for another reason. Now that the war was turning in favor of the Americans it appeared that he would be able to fulfill his ambition of going to Andover Academy in preparation for attending Harvard College.

Johnny's father was a Harvard graduate, so on

the summer day that the boy told his parents of his plans he expected them to be pleased. Instead, Mr. and Mrs. Adams just stared at him.

Several days later Abigail Adams had a talk with her oldest son. She explained that the Continental Congress wanted Mr. Adams to return to Paris for further negotiations. Both she and Mr. Adams thought that Johnny, with his knowledge of French, would be a tremendous help to his father on this trip.

Johnny was stunned by this news, but he agreed to go. Two months later, on November 13, 1779, John Quincy set out with his father and also his younger brother Charles on what was to be the greatest adventure of Johnny's long life. This time the British left their ship alone, but in the middle of the ocean the vessel sprang a leak that threatened to sink it.

Thanks to constant pumping by the crew and passengers, the vessel was able to reach the northwest coast of Spain. From there the three Adamses started out by carriage on the more than twelve-hundred-mile trip to Paris. At times, Johnny, his little brother, and their father had to go by mule across the snow-covered mountains. Mr. Adams, who was nearly forty-five years old, did not enjoy this mode of travel. Johnny and Charles, however, loved the adventure and the scenery. And for Johnny, there was another benefit to the trip through

Spain. By the time they left the country, he could speak Spanish.

Upon their arrival in Paris in February 1780 Johnny and his brother were enrolled in school while their father went about his diplomatic tasks. By now Great Britain was losing the war against the United States, and Mr. Adams hoped to negotiate a peace treaty with the former mother country. The English weren't yet ready to concede defeat, however, and so the negotiations had to be suspended.

John Adams was then named minister to the Netherlands, and in that capacity he took the two boys to the city of Amsterdam with him. While their father worked to secure a huge loan from the Netherlands for the Americans, Charles and Johnny attended public school in Amsterdam. Johnny was such an outstanding student that when he was still just thirteen years old he enrolled at the University of Leiden, the most famous university in all of Europe at the time.

Johnny had been attending the university for several months when an American diplomat named Francis Dana came to speak to Mr. Adams. Dana was about to make the first American diplomatic trip to Russia. At that time French was the language spoken at the Russian court of Empress Catherine the Great, and Dana wanted Johnny to serve as his interpreter and secretary. Mr. Adams gave his permission, and when Johnny heard the proposal he agreed to go.

On July 7, 1781 — four days before Johnny's fourteenth birthday — he and Mr. Dana set out from Amsterdam by carriage. They were bound for the Russian capital of St. Petersburg (now Leningrad), a trip of more than two thousand miles at that time. John Quincy wrote to his father that this long journey made a great impression on him. When he observed Europeans working like slaves for landlords and kings, he had a new appreciation of the meaning of freedom.

As soon as they arrived in Russia in late August, John Quincy wrote a letter to his father to let him know that he was safe. Then he and Mr. Dana went to work. Their goal was to convince Catherine the Great to recognize the United States as a sovereign country.

In order to gain an audience with the empress they first had to speak to a multitude of diplomats and politicians. John Quincy wrote letters in French to the Russian officials for Mr. Dana. Then, when Mr. Dana met with the officials, the fourteen-year-old served as translator. After working all day translating letters and conversations, John Quincy often attended a ball or banquet at night, and also found time to study history, literature, and the Greek, Latin, German, and Russian languages during his lengthy stay in St. Petersburg.

After John Quincy Adams and Francis Dana had been in Russia for more than a year, it became apparent that Catherine the Great did not want to meet with them. Although the United States had won the Revolutionary War in October 1781, the empress did not want to risk antagonizing Britain by recognizing the new country. Mr. Dana remained in Russia to keep trying, but in October 1782 John Quincy Adams set out from St. Petersburg on the long return trip to the Netherlands.

John Quincy's return took six months because of the winter weather. On the way, the fifteen-year-old youth stopped in cities in Sweden, Norway, and Denmark. He spoke to merchants in those countries and convinced many of them to start doing business with the United States.

When John Quincy arrived in the Netherlands in April 1783, he learned that his father was in Paris discussing the peace treaty between the United States and Britain. John Quincy then went to Paris and there worked as his father's private secretary. He attended all the negotiations and made copies of the peace documents for his father and the other two American diplomats, Benjamin Franklin and John Jay. The agreement created by the American and British diplomats, called the Treaty of Paris, was signed on September 3, 1783, and officially ended the Revolutionary War.

By this time Charles Adams had returned home,

but John Quincy Adams stayed on with his father in Europe until the summer of 1785. When he finally returned to the United States, eighteen-year-old John Quincy Adams had many achievements behind him. In addition to having served as secretary to the first American diplomat in Russia and having aided his father during the Treaty of Paris discussions, John Quincy Adams had become familiar with more parts of Europe than any other American of his time.

All this experience was put to good use in his later life. After serving as United States senator, United States minister to the Netherlands, Russia, and Great Britain, and secretary of state, John Quincy Adams was elected sixth President of the United States. He and John Adams, the second President, are the only father and son who have both held the highest office in the United States.

After his term as President John Quincy Adams was elected to the federal House of Representatives from his home state of Massachusetts. For the last seventeen years of his life he served in the House, where, among other things, he tried to end slavery. John Quincy Adams, who had worked for his country almost continually since the age of fourteen, suffered a fatal stroke at the age of eighty while at his desk in the House of Representatives.

Sacagawea

(1789?–1812?)

Sacagawea was sleeping in a skin tepee with her family near the three forks of the Missouri River in what is now western Montana when she was suddenly awakened by shouts. Seconds later the eleven-year-old girl was on her feet and running out of the tent with her brother Cameahwait and the rest of her family. Outside, Sacagawea saw that a large number of raiders on horseback were knocking down the tents of her people, shooting many of the fleeing adults with arrows, and taking away some of the women and children as prisoners.

As Sacagawea ran toward the river, she could still hear the screams of her injured and dying relatives and friends. She had reached the river and was wading across at a shallow spot when a man on horseback thundered into the water and pulled her onto his horse. The terrified girl fought, but the man was too strong and forced her to ride away with him.

Sacagawea, a Shoshone Indian whose name meant "Bird Woman," had been born about 1789 in a village in what is now Idaho. Her people were nomads who moved about as they gathered roots and seeds and hunted animals with their bows and arrows. This way of life was ending now for the young girl on this night in the fall of 1800. The man on horseback, who was a Minnetaree Indian, took Sacagawea back to his village in what is now North Dakota and made her his slave. The other Shoshone women and children who had been kidnapped that night were also enslaved by various Minnetarees.

Little is known about Sacagawea's captivity, but it is reasonable to assume that she hoped to be rescued by her people. They weren't the ones who finally took Sacagawea away, however. One day not long after her capture a French trader named Toussaint Charbonneau arrived at the Minnetaree village. Besides trading with the Minnetarees for animal furs, Charbonneau gambled with them. Charbonneau entered the tent of the man who owned Sacagawea and a short time later he had won the Indian girl.

Charbonneau took Sacagawea with him and "married" her, just as he "married" many other Indian girls during his long life. They weren't married by a minister or a justice of the peace. Charbonneau merely said, "You are my wife," and that was that. Charbonneau took Sacagawea into the country of the Mandan Indians, where he had another wife, and settled near present-day Bismarck, North Dakota. Really more of a slave than a wife, Sacagawea was put to work making clothes and harvesting the beans, corn, and squash grown by the Mandans in the fertile Missouri River valley.

One day in the fall of 1804 Captain Meriwether Lewis and Captain William Clark, two American explorers, arrived in the Mandan country. They had come from St. Louis and were partway through an exploring trip that was supposed to take them through what is now the northwestern United States all the way to the Pacific Ocean. Lewis and Clark built Fort Mandan out of logs near the village where Sacagawea and Charbonneau lived. Charbonneau heard that Lewis and Clark needed interpreters — particularly one who could speak to the Shoshones, from whom they hoped to buy horses and obtain help in crossing the mountains. Charbonneau brought Sacagawea to the fort, and soon both of them were asked to accompany the expedition.

Charbonneau and Sacagawea spent the winter of 1804–1805 with the expedition at Fort Mandan. There, in February 1805, the sixteen-year-old Sacagawea gave birth to her first child. Charbonneau named him Jean-Baptiste, but Sacagawea called him Pomp — a Shoshone name meaning "leader."

Two months later, on the afternoon of April 7, 1805, Sacagawea walked out of Fort Mandan with Pomp strapped to her back and Charbonneau at her side. As she climbed into the large white pirogue (a dugout canoe) and sat down, Sacagawea must have been very excited. In a few minutes she would be heading in the direction of her own people.

The men finished boarding the two pirogues and the six smaller canoes. At four o'clock in the afternoon Captain Lewis and Captain Clark, both of whom would also be traveling in the white pirogue, stood up and signaled for the boats to be launched. A few seconds later, as the crowd on shore cheered, the eight vessels, containing three dozen people, thousands of pounds of supplies, and Lewis's huge Newfoundland dog, Scammon, departed.

The expedition traveled about fifteen miles a day. As they moved westward up the Missouri River, Sacagawea did her best to keep her baby happy.

She knew that the men — who were hunters, fighters, and frontiersmen — were not pleased about having a woman, let alone a baby, along on the trip, and that they might get annoyed if Pomp cried. Captain Lewis, who liked to walk along the shore with the 140-pound Scammon, paid little attention to Sacagawea and Charbonneau. But the red-haired Captain Clark, who had come from a large family, took an immediate liking to Pomp. Sometimes before they went to sleep in the big leather tent Clark would take Pomp on his knee and sing songs to him.

On their third day out of Fort Mandan, Sacagawea performed her first major service for the expedition. At dinner that evening she saw that the men were displeased with the dry meat and cornmeal that they were being served. Sacagawea disappeared into the woods and returned with a quantity of roots, which she then cooked. Most of the men liked the roots, which Captain Clark called "wild artichokes." After that, Captain Clark began inviting Sacagawea and Charbonneau to walk with him along the shore. The strawberries, gooseberries, plums, camas roots, white apples, fennel, and wild onions that the girl gathered spiced up the men's diet and also provided them with necessary vitamins they would have otherwise lacked.

A little more than a month out of Fort Mandan, Sacagawea helped the expedition during a major crisis. On the cold, foggy afternoon of May 14, 1805, several of the men who usually traveled in the white pirogue were out hunting a grizzly bear. Lewis and Clark were walking along the shore noting the geography, flora, and fauna of the region. Charbonneau was steering the boat, which contained himself, Sacagawea, Pomp, and several other persons. Suddenly a strong gust of wind struck the sail broadside and tipped the pirogue so that it began to fill with water.

The big, bearded Charbonneau, who couldn't swim, began shouting for God to save him. As the pirogue continued to fill with water, the supplies — including medicine, scientific instruments, and goods for trading — began to float away. Looking toward shore, Sacagawea saw that she could swim there with Pomp on her back if the boat sank. She then calmly reached out and caught the supplies that were floating away. Meanwhile, several men used kettles to bail the water out of the pirogue, which they soon managed to right. In the journal he kept of the expedition, Captain Lewis described how grateful he and Clark were to Sacagawea for her actions during this crisis:

> The Indian woman to whom I ascribe equal fortitude and resolution, with any person on-board at the time of the accident, caught and

preserved most of the light articles which were washed overboard.

Each day the trip westward brought new problems. When the travelers approached rapids and waterfalls, they had to carry their boats and supplies around them. At times the voyagers didn't have sufficient food and often many of them were sick. They were assaulted by mosquitoes, which turned their bodies into masses of red sores, and they even had fights with grizzlies. One of the closest calls occurred in June 1805 when Sacagawea, Pomp, Clark, and Charbonneau were nearly swept away by a flash flood. They had barely climbed out of a ravine when it filled with ten feet of raging water.

In June the expedition reached what is now western Montana. Sacagawea was spotting familiar landmarks by this time, and she even showed the men the spot where she had been captured while fleeing from her village. By now she must have been thinking that she could encounter her people any minute — if any of them were still alive.

By early August, when the expedition neared present-day Idaho, everyone was maintaining a sharp lookout for the Shoshones. In an effort to find the Indians, Lewis and several other men left the main party and explored several trails made by the Native Americans. On August 13, 1805, near what is now the Montana–Idaho border, Captain Lewis encountered three Shoshones, who led him and his men into their camp.

After the white Americans and the Native Americans exchanged presents, Captain Lewis used sign language to communicate with the Shoshone chief, whose name was Cameahwait. Lewis explained that he was part of a larger expedition and convinced the Indians to accompany him to meet it.

As the Indians walked with the whites toward the main body of the expedition, Captain Lewis sensed trouble. The Indians, who suspected that they were being led into an ambush, began talking angrily to Cameahwait. The situation seemed very dangerous to Captain Lewis, who knew that he and his few men would have no chance if the hundred Shoshones with them decided to attack.

When the main body of the expedition came into view and the Indians saw the large group of white men with guns, trouble seemed even more likely. This was a crucial moment in United States history. At the time, both the United States and Great Britain claimed ownership of what is now the northwestern United States. If Lewis and Clark could successfully complete their exploration, the American claim to this land would be strengthened. If they failed, the way might be opened for the British to add this region to their vast Canadian holdings.

When some of the Indians reached for their bows, it appeared that the Lewis and Clark Expedition was about to be engaged in a full-scale battle. But then suddenly the Indians spotted a young Shoshone woman with a baby on her back amidst all the white men. Seeing that these Indians were her own people, Sacagawea placed her fingers in her mouth as a sign of recognition and began to leap up and down and yell joyfully. In the journals kept by members of the expedition, the moment when Sacagawea spotted her brother Cameahwait was described as follows:

> Sacagawea was . . . beginning to interpret, when, in the person of Cameahwait, she recognized her brother. She instantly jumped up, and ran and embraced him, throwing over him her blanket, and weeping profusely. The chief himself was moved, though not in the same degree. After some conversation between them she . . . attempted to interpret for us, but her new situation seemed to overpower her, and she was frequently interrupted by her tears. After the council was finished the unfortunate woman learned that all her family were dead except two brothers, one of whom was absent, and a son of her eldest sister, a small boy. . . .

Sacagawea had to pull herself together, because it was her job to serve as translator while Lewis and Clark purchased the much-needed horses from the chief. Sacagawea translated her brother's words into French, and then Charbonneau converted the French into English for the two captains.

During the next several days the Indians and the explorers celebrated together with food, dances, and songs. But one night, when Sacagawea was sitting by the campfire near Cameahwait, she heard her brother say something startling to another Indian. As part of his deal with Lewis and Clark, Cameahwait had promised to help the expedition carry supplies across the mountains. Now Cameahwait said that he was going to go back on his word. His people needed food, and he was planning to lead them out of the camp and go buffalo hunting without letting Lewis and Clark know about it.

It must have been difficult for Sacagawea to decide what to do. Without her brother's help, the expedition might not be able to make it across the mountains. On the other hand, if she told of her brother's plans, her people might despise her. Finally she decided that, although the Shoshone were her people, she was working for Lewis and Clark and owed them her loyalty. Sacagawea told Charbonneau about what her brother had said, and Charbonneau told Captain Lewis about it. When Captain Lewis confronted Cameahwait with this information, the chief agreed to provide the help he'd promised for the mountain crossing. There is no record of how Cameahwait reacted to the fact that his sister had informed on him.

The remainder of the trip to the Pacific Ocean was very hard. Although it was just September, snow had already fallen in the Rocky Mountains, and the horses, which were carrying the supplies, came close to tumbling down the sides of the icy canyon trails. It was difficult for the men to walk through the snow day after day and even more difficult for Sacagawea, who had to carry Pomp, wrapped up in a blanket.

Several more times on the way to the Pacific the expedition encountered Indians. The Native Americans had cause to be suspicious of the white men, who had been seizing their lands in various parts of North America for many years. Probably the expedition would have been attacked by Indians several times had it not been for the presence of the young Indian woman with the baby in her arms. Clark referred to this in his journal when he wrote: "A woman with a party of men is a token of peace."

On October 16, 1805, the expedition reached the Columbia — a river that flows through what is now the northwestern United States and southwestern Canada. There were so many rapids and whirlpools along the Columbia that the travelers had to carry their boats much of the time. There was also a tremendous amount of rainfall, which kept the travelers cold, damp, and often sick. Nevertheless, on November 17 the Lewis and Clark Expedition reached its goal — the mouth of the Columbia River at the Pacific Ocean. They built their winter quarters, called Fort Clatsop, near what is now Astoria, Oregon.

During the long winter at Fort Clatsop Sacagawea made hundreds of moccasins for the men to wear on the trip home. During this winter she also showed that she had changed since the April afternoon when she had meekly stepped into the pirogue at Fort Mandan. One day in late December 1805, some local Indians reported that there was a monstrous whale on the beach. When it became evident that Captain Clark expected her to stay in the fort and make moccasins while the men trekked off to see the whale, Sacagawea spoke up. In his journal, Captain Clark wrote that Sacagawea complained about the injustice of this:

> Monday, 6th of January, 1806   The last evening, Shabono and his Indian woman was very impatient to go with me. She observed that She had traveled a long way with us to See the great waters, and that now that monstrous fish was also to be Seen, She thought it very hard that She could not be permitted to See either.

Realizing that he was being unfair, Clark changed his mind and took Sacagawea along.

On March 23, 1806, the expedition left Fort Clatsop and headed for home. As they rowed along rivers and crossed mountains, the voyagers had more bouts with hunger and illness. Finally, in mid-August of 1806 they reached Fort Mandan. There Sacagawea, Pomp, and Charbonneau left the expedition and returned home. For his part in serving as interpreter, Charbonneau was paid about five hundred dollars. Sacagawea received no pay for her valuable services.

Historians have spent much time and effort trying to determine what became of Sacagawea following the expedition. On December 20, 1812, the clerk at a Missouri River trading post wrote: "This evening the wife of Charbonneau, a Snake [Shoshone] squaw, died of a putrid fever." Some historians think that the young woman who died was Sacagawea, while others say that it was one of Charbonneau's other wives. A woman who said that she was Sacagawea, and who was thought by many to be her, died on a Wyoming Indian reservation at the age of nearly one hundred in 1884. It is still debated as to whether this was the real Sacagawea or just someone claiming to be the famous guide.

Mary Anning

(1799–1847)

Mary Anning lived with her family on Bridge Street in the little town of Lyme Regis on England's southern coast. Mary's father, Richard Anning, was a carpenter by trade, but he had an interesting hobby that consumed much of his and his children's time. He liked to take Mary and her older brother, Joseph, out to the cliffs along the ocean and search for what people called "curiosities."

Actually, these curiosities were fossils — remains of ancient plants and animals. The Annings would sell the curiosities to summer vacationers who came to Lyme Regis to bathe in the ocean. In the early 1800s people were becoming very interested in science, and each summer the wealthy vacationers from London and the other big cities bought most of the Annings' fossils.

All her life, Mary was to remember her childhood up to the age of eleven as a happy time. She loved digging for fossils of fish and other ancient sea creatures with her father and Joseph, and in the summer she enjoyed standing outside their cottage and selling them to the tourists.

When she was eleven years old, however, there was an abrupt change in Mary Anning's life. Her father died of tuberculosis. In addition to feeling grief-stricken, the Annings suddenly found themselves impoverished. Fourteen-year-old Joseph obtained a job working for an upholsterer, but he brought in so little money that there were times when the family didn't have enough to eat. Mary had gone to school up to this time, but now she had to quit.

Mary Anning continued her fossil-hunting excursions, usually by herself, but sometimes with Joseph. One afternoon when Mary was returning from the cliffs with her basket in hand, she met a wealthy lady who asked to see her curiosities. The woman gave the eleven-year-old girl half a crown for a fossil shell known as an ammonite. Realizing that she could help her family with their money problems, Mary

Anning began spending more time than ever collecting fossils, which she then sold to her townspeople and to vacationers in Lyme Regis.

One day when Mary was out at the oceanside, a stray dog suddenly appeared and stayed by her side as she worked. Mary's mother allowed her to keep the little black-and-white dog. Mary named the dog Tray, and from then on he always kept her company when she went curiosity hunting.

Occasionally Joseph went curiosity hunting by himself and brought home fossils that were placed on the table alongside Mary's. One day Joseph brought home a most unusual fossil — a tooth-filled skull more than two feet long. Joseph, Mary, and everyone else who saw it thought that the fossil belonged to a prehistoric crocodile. Hoping to find the rest of the skeleton, Mary asked Joseph to show her the place where he had found the skull.

Over the next few months Mary came back again and again to the place where her brother had found the giant skull, but to no avail. Then, one night early in 1811, when Mary was nearly twelve years old, there was a tremendous storm. During the night, the rain and the wind uncovered the rest of the skeleton. When she and Tray ran down to the beach in the morning, Mary spotted the largest skeleton she had ever seen, sticking out of the cliffside. Mary took her hammer and chisel out of her basket and carefully tapped away at the dirt and rock, as she had been taught by her father. When she had uncovered the rib cage, she saw that the skeleton was monstrous — more than fifteen feet long.

Realizing that she could not uncover the entire skeleton by herself, Mary ran into town. Soon, possibly in a tavern, she obtained the services of several strong men. Under Mary's direction, the men carefully dug the huge skeleton out of the cliff. Once the skeleton was freed from the cliff, Mary offered the workmen an additional fee to carry it home for her.

The workmen, accompanied by the eleven-year-old girl, must have made a strange-looking procession as they carried the hundred-million-year-old bones through the streets of Lyme Regis. Although her reaction isn't recorded, we can imagine Mrs. Anning's surprise when she heard a knock at the door and looked out to see the gigantic skeleton! Because of its great size, Mary probably had to leave the skeleton outside on the street very close to her house.

During the next several weeks scientists throughout England heard about the strange skeleton that had been found by a young girl in Lyme Regis. Many came to the town to see it for themselves. Soon it was determined that Mary had uncovered the first complete skeleton of Ichthyosaurus (meaning "fish lizard"), a fishlike reptile that had lived during the age of the dinosaurs. A wealthy man in Lyme Regis bought the Ichthyosaurus skeleton for twenty-three pounds.

The Ichthyosaurus skeleton was placed in a museum and eventually made its way into the British Museum in London. As for Mary Anning, her name became known throughout England and beyond. Well-known scientists came to Lyme Regis to buy her fossils, and thus helped her become one of the first persons to turn fossil collecting into a full-time, paying profession.

As an adult, Mary Anning made more important discoveries. In 1824, at the age of twenty-five, she discovered a nearly complete skeleton of Plesiosaurus, a huge sea serpent that lived two hundred million years ago. Although Plesiosaurus bones had been found previously, this was the first essentially intact skeleton of the animal to be discovered. In 1828 Mary Anning made her third great discovery, the remains of a huge flying reptile called a Pterodactyl, which had lived about a hundred and fifty million years ago. Among her other major discoveries were a second Plesiosaurus and a second Ichthyosaurus.

Mary Anning made enough money selling her fossils to move her mother, brother, and herself into a pleasant home on Broad Street. She converted part of the house into a shop, and there she sold fossils to everyone who was interested, including the king of Saxony and Dr. Gideon Mantell, the first discoverer of dinosaur bones. The children of Lyme Regis also liked to drop into "The Fossil Woman's" shop to spend their pocket money on ammonites and other inexpensive fossils.

One of the few descriptions we have of Mary Anning was provided by Nellie Waring, who as a child frequented the fossil shop and later wrote about her in a memoir called *Peeps into an Old Playground: Memories of the Past:*

> Miss Anning "The Fossil Woman" lived in Broad Street, in a house with a small shop front. . . . There lived this very timid, very unpretending, very patient, and very celebrated woman, the discoverer of the Ichthyosaurus and of other fossil remains which were living animals before the Deluge. We, as children, had large dealings with Miss Anning, our pocket-money was freely spent on the little Ammonites which she washed and burnished till they shone like metal, and on stones which took our childish fancy. She would serve us with the sweetest temper, bearing with all our little fancies and never finding us too troublesome as we turned over her trays of curiosities. . . . She must have been poor enough, for her little shop was scantily furnished, and her own dress always of the very plainest, she was very thin and had a high forehead, and

large eyes which seemed to have a kindly consideration for her little customers. There was "Mrs. Anning the Fossilwoman's mother" too, a very old lady in a mob cap and large white apron, who sometimes came with feeble steps into the shop to help us in our selection.

Over the years Mary Anning had several near-accidents as she climbed about on the cliffs of Lyme Regis, but it was cancer that ended her life at the age of forty-eight in 1847. At the edge of the cliff at Lyme Regis there is a church, and it was there that some of Mary Anning's friends placed a window and a plaque in memory of "The Fossil Woman." The plaque reads:

> This window is sacred to the memory of Mary Anning, of this parish, who died March 9th, 1847, and is erected by the Vicar of Lyme and some of the members of the Geological Society of London, in commemoration of her usefulness in furthering the science of geology, as also of her benevolence of heart and integrity of life.

Even more meaningful memorials are the many fossils found by Mary Anning that can be seen in the British Museum and other museums throughout the world.

Zerah Colburn

(1804–1839)

In the summer of 1810, when Zerah Colburn was not quite six years old, he attended school for six weeks in his hometown of Cabot, Vermont. Zerah's teacher taught him and his classmates to count and to do simple arithmetic problems. He showed them the letters, taught them to read simple words, and no doubt explained that James Madison was President of the United States and that there were seventeen states.

No one seems to have noticed that Zerah was different from any other average student during those six weeks in school. But shortly after school ended for the summer, Zerah was sitting in his father's workshed playing with some wood chips while Mr. Colburn made a cabinet. Moving the chips about, the freckled, red-haired Zerah said, "Five times seven are thirty-five. Six times eight are forty-eight. Seven times —"

Zerah's father, Abiah Colburn, listened in amazement for a while. Then he put down his tools and asked, "And what is thirteen times ninety-seven?"

Almost immediately the boy answered, "One thousand, two hundred and sixty-one."

His father then asked Zerah several more difficult problems, all of which the boy answered correctly. Zerah was still astonishing his father when a neighbor rode up on horseback. For the next few minutes Zerah rattled off answers nearly as fast as the neighbor posed the problems.

The neighbor spread the word about the quiet boy, who had heretofore been considered the most "backward" of the seven Colburn children. During the next few days people rode up to the Colburn farm just to hear Zerah "cipher." When Mr. Colburn heard his neighbors proclaim the boy a genius, it occurred to him that a fortune could be made by exhibiting Zerah. Because their little farm couldn't support the family, Mr. Colburn had to work as a cabinetmaker to earn some extra money. The prospect of making a fortune from Zerah's talent was extremely tantalizing to him.

Several weeks later Mr. Colburn arranged for Zerah to give a mathematical demonstration for the benefit of the Vermont state lawmakers. On an October morning Abiah and Zerah Colburn traveled twenty miles on horseback to Montpelier, the Vermont capital, and walked into the new three-story wooden State House. Mr. Colburn introduced Zerah to the lawmakers and then challenged them to try to stump him.

The lawmakers asked Zerah more and more difficult problems and were amazed by his correct answers. Then they came up with a few trick questions. "Which is more, twice twenty-five, or twice five plus twenty?" asked one lawmaker. "Which is more, six dozen dozen or half a dozen dozen?" asked another. After Zerah answered both questions correctly, another lawmaker asked, "How many black beans will make five white ones?"

Zerah had to take a little longer for that one, but he finally said, "Five, sir, if you skin them."

The lawmakers laughed and said, "Bravo!" and "Thank you for bringing him, Mr. Colburn!" Abiah Colburn was disappointed, however, because he had hoped that the lawmakers would suggest some way to make money from Zerah's talent.

Mr. Colburn now decided that he should show Zerah to the world, and that the best place to start was Boston, one of the leading intellectual centers of the United States. Mrs. Colburn packed up some clothes and food, and then Zerah and his father headed for the Massachusetts capital.

Since it was on the way, Abiah Colburn stopped with Zerah at Dartmouth College in Hanover, New Hampshire. There they met with Dr. John Wheelock, the Dartmouth president.

Dr. Wheelock had Zerah do some difficult problems and then posed a very difficult one. "What is the cube root of two hundred sixty-eight million, three hundred thirty-six thousand, one hundred and twenty-five?" asked the Dartmouth president. Several seconds later Zerah, who had only recently been taught the names of the very large numbers by his father, answered: "Six hundred and forty-five."

After conversing with the boy for a while and learning that he couldn't read yet, Dr. Wheelock made Mr. Colburn an offer. If Abiah would leave Zerah in Hanover, Dr. Wheelock would see to it that the boy received a complete education with no expense to the Colburn family. Unfortunately, Abiah Colburn turned down this offer. By doing so, he deprived Zerah of an excellent educational opportunity.

Once they arrived in Boston, Mr. Colburn rented a hall, where, for a few pennies, people could come and ask the six-year-old to perform problems. Thanks mainly to the autobiography *(A Memoir of*

Zerah Colburn) that Zerah later wrote, we know some of the questions he was asked.

"How many seconds are there in two thousand years?" asked one Bostonian.

"There are seven hundred and thirty thousand days," Zerah answered, and then paused to continue his calculations. "Seventeen million, five hundred and twenty thousand hours . . . one billion, fifty-one million, and two hundred thousand minutes . . . and sixty-three billion and seventy-two million seconds."

"Suppose I have a seven-acre cornfield in which there are seventeen rows to each acre, sixty-four hills to each row, eight ears on a hill, and a hundred and fifty kernels on an ear. How many kernels are in the cornfield?"

"Nine million, one hundred thirty-nine thousand, two hundred," answered the child calculator.

In Boston — and everywhere else that Zerah was to go — there was one question he was always asked: "How do you get your answers?"

Because he didn't know, Zerah always responded, "God put it into my head and I cannot put it into yours."

While Zerah was in Boston, he came to the attention of a group of wealthy men that included Josiah Quincy, a lawyer who later became mayor of Boston and then president of Harvard University. These men concluded that it was wrong for

Zerah to be exhibited like a freak and that the boy should be educated so that he could do something useful with his talent. These prominent Bostonians made Mr. Colburn an offer. If he would leave Zerah with them, they would educate the boy at the finest schools and universities. Realizing that Mr. Colburn was money-hungry, they offered him a twenty-five-hundred-dollar bonus just for agreeing to let them educate Zerah. Still dreaming of making a fortune from his son, Mr. Colburn turned down their offer and returned home with Zerah.

Shortly afterward, Zerah and his father set out on a tour of the East Coast, which included stops in such places as New York City, Philadelphia, Washington, D.C., the Virginia cities of Fredericksburg, Richmond, and Norfolk, and Charleston in South Carolina. The first thing Abiah and Zerah would do upon their arrival in a town would be to rent a hotel room. Sometimes Mr. Colburn would manage to hook Zerah up with a traveling circus or road show, and then the boy would do his arithmetic tricks right next to the tattooed lady or the sword swallower. But most of the time Mr. Colburn would have to rent a hall, where people would pay to ask Zerah questions.

The problem was that Mr. Colburn hadn't anticipated the high cost of traveling about the country. The nickels and dimes that they took in were more than eaten up by their bills for hotels, meals, and hall rentals. By the time the Colburns reached Charleston, most of their money was gone, and so they returned to Boston.

If Mr. Colburn had been realistic, he would have given up his idea of making money from Zerah's amazing talent. Instead, he asked the prominent Bostonians who had offered to educate his son to send the two of them to Europe. The Bostonians provided the money, and then Zerah and Abiah returned to their home in Vermont for a short visit with their family.

People who have written about Zerah Colburn have usually referred to Abiah as a greedy and ignorant man who was continually trying to exploit his son. In his autobiography, however, Zerah loyally defended his father and never complained about the constant travel and exhibitions that marked his boyhood.

On a spring day in 1812, seven-year-old Zerah and his father sailed from home. After a stormy thirty-eight-day Atlantic crossing they arrived in England, where for the most part they were treated like royalty. The only problem was that the War of 1812 broke out between England and the United States on almost the exact day that Zerah and his father arrived in London. Because some English people had ill feelings toward Americans, Zerah sometimes affected a Russian accent when he gave his demonstrations.

Zerah was showered with shillings at his public shows, and he was also given the chance to perform in front of royalty and university professors. Now at the very height of his mathematical powers, Zerah so astonished his audiences that he was referred to as the "Eighth Wonder of the World."

At one demonstration in late July 1813 the Duke of Cambridge asked Zerah: "How many seconds have there been since the birth of Christ?"

After thinking for a few seconds, nine-year-old Zerah answered: "Fifty-seven billion, two hundred thirty-four million, three hundred and eighty-four thousand."

"What is the square of nine hundred ninety-nine thousand, nine hundred and ninety-nine?" asked William Wilberforce, a famous English lawmaker.

Evidently all those nines caused him some problems, because at first Zerah said he couldn't do that one. When prodded to try, Zerah concentrated and then answered: "Nine hundred ninety-nine billion, nine hundred ninety-eight million — and one!"

Before and since the time of Zerah Colburn, human computers have occasionally appeared in various parts of the world. Most have been young boys whose powers of computation disappeared in adulthood. When Zerah Colburn was presented before them, London's university professors wanted to determine something that hasn't been answered to this day. How do these mathematical wizards arrive at their answers? Zerah couldn't explain his method to them, and the professors couldn't figure out how he did it. The only conclusion the professors could make was that somehow Zerah's brain was able to function as a calculating machine.

Despite Zerah's popularity in England, the money he earned during the two years there barely paid for his and his father's hotel room. Growing desperate, Mr. Colburn then took Zerah to Paris. Zerah continued to astound his audiences, which included Pierre-Simon, Marquis de Laplace, who was a famous mathematician and astronomer, and John Quincy Adams, who later became the sixth President of the United States. Both Laplace and Adams urged Abiah Colburn to see to his son's education. John Quincy Adams mentioned this in an entry he made in his diary shortly after meeting Zerah in Paris in spring of 1815:

[March 2, 1815] Zerah Colburn came this morning with his father and another man. . . . The boy was born 1st September 1804 and has, it would seem, a faculty for the composition and decomposition of numbers of inspiration. His father says he discovered it in him August 1810 when he was not quite 6 years old, and had never learned the first rules of arithmetic. Even now he cannot do a common sum in the rule of three, but he can by a mental process of his own extract the roots of any power or number and name the factors by which any given number is produced. I asked him what it was that first turned his attention to the combination of numbers. He said he could not tell. . . . Zerah is certainly an astonishing and promising boy; but if his promise is ever to realize anything, the sooner his father commits him to the tuition of the Polytechnic School the better.

Zerah did attend school in Paris for a while, but unfortunately the Colburns happened to be in Paris during the Napoleonic wars, a time when the French had more serious topics on their minds than a boy calculator. The audiences in Paris were small, a disastrous occurrence considering that Mr. Colburn had rented an eleven-room mansion in order to attract attention.

Early in 1816, after about a year and a half in France, Zerah returned to London with his father, who was quite heavily in debt. The audiences were dwindling because Zerah was no longer a cute little boy, and Mr. Colburn now accepted the Earl of Bristol's offer to send Zerah to Westminster School. For almost four years Zerah studied at this school, where he was a very good student but displayed no remarkable mental ability.

By the time Zerah was fifteen, his calculating ability was rapidly diminishing. Possibly because Zerah was used to performing in front of audiences, Mr. Colburn decided that his son should embark upon an acting career. Zerah managed to get parts in several plays, but he displayed no acting talent. The biggest disaster in Zerah's acting career occurred when Zerah and his father went to Ireland to look for theater work. While in Belfast they ran out of money and had to walk seventy miles to their next engagement in Londonderry. Zerah also tried to write plays and operate a private school, but without success.

In 1823, when Zerah was nineteen, he obtained a job calculating the positions of stars for a British scientist. Zerah loved this job, which was the only one he ever had in which he made practical use of his mathematical ability. In fact, Zerah might have gone on to become a famous astronomer except for another occurrence. In 1824 Abiah Colburn became very ill with tuberculosis and called Zerah to his bedside. With his last breath Abiah begged Zerah to return home to the family they had left twelve years earlier.

After his father's death Zerah gave up his astronomy job and sailed back to the United States. All he had to show for twelve years in Europe was a fifty-dollar gift from the English Earl of Bristol.

Once home, Zerah found that his mother and

brothers and sisters had managed to keep the farm going. For the rest of his short life Zerah Colburn worked as a schoolteacher, a traveling preacher, and then a professor of languages. He married a Vermont woman, and they had six children. By the time he reached his twenties Zerah Colburn, who had once been called the "Eighth Wonder of the World," had lost his calculating ability almost completely.

Louis Braille

(1809–1852)

Three-year-old Louis Braille was playing, as he often did, in his father's workshop. Louis's father was a harness maker in their hometown of Coupvray, France, just twenty-five miles outside Paris. While his father made saddles and other horseback-riding equipment, Louis, who was the youngest of the family's four children, liked to play with the extra leather scraps. Sometimes Louis's father even let him use a spare tool, such as a dull knife or an awl, a pointed instrument used for punching holes in the leather.

On this particular day in early 1812, Louis was playing with the tools and a leather scrap while his father worked on a new set of reins for a neighboring lawyer. To complete his design, Louis wanted to punch holes in the leather scrap. Because he was only three years old, he had to stab fiercely at the leather with the awl each time he wanted to make another hole. He was doing that when suddenly the instrument glanced off the tough leather and pierced his left eye. The next thing Louis knew he was being held and comforted by his father and also by his mother, who had come running when she heard the boy's screams. Finally the hysterical parents slowed the bleeding and then bandaged and patched the eye.

Terrible though the injury was, the Brailles hoped at first that the sight in Louis's left eye would be restored. Although they were not wealthy, Simon and Monique Braille spared no expense in taking their son to various doctors. Today at least one of Louis Braille's eyes would have been saved. But in those days doctors were helpless in the face of many kinds of injuries and illnesses, and they had no knowledge of germs. Because Louis's injured eye was not kept clean, an infection set in and soon spread to his good eye. Although Louis recovered from the infection, he was left totally blind. Too young to understand what had happened, Louis only knew that he couldn't get around the house without the cane that his father had carved for him.

In those days, the blind were often thrown out

of their households at an early age, many to become beggars. Some of the luckier ones were given menial jobs, such as shoveling coal or carrying things all day like human mules, in exchange for a daily meal and a place to sleep. Simon and Monique Braille, however, had the means — and the love — to care for their son. They vowed that Louis would never be cut off from the world because of his blindness. His father, who felt responsible for the accident, spent much time every day with Louis and always described to him how everything looked.

As the two of them walked through the fields on the way to Coupvray's one-room schoolhouse, Louis's father would describe the countryside, the town, and the people they encountered. Then he would ask, "What do you think of the weather today, Louis?"

If he could feel the warmth of the sun shining on his face, the thin, pale boy would answer, "The sun is shining and it is warm." Then he would ask, "What color is the sky?"

"As blue as can be," his father would answer. Louis struggled to understand blue, but he had been blinded at too early an age to remember colors. All his life he wondered what people meant when they said something was blue or red or yellow.

All six hundred people in Coupvray became familiar with the sight of the harness maker walking up the road with his little blind son. "Here comes little Louis," they would say, whenever they heard the tap-tap of his cane. Louis captured people's attention for another reason besides his blindness. He was extremely intelligent. He spent many hours talking to the schoolmaster and to the village priest about music, poetry, biblical stories, and geography.

By Louis's tenth birthday his brother and oldest sister were married and out of the house and his other sister was soon to be wed. The Brailles now faced a problem. In those days school was a luxury reserved mainly for the rich. Few children — particularly blind children — attended school beyond the age of ten. The Brailles wondered what their blind son would do with his life.

One day Louis heard from the schoolmaster about a special school for the blind in Paris. He told his parents he wanted to go to that school. The village priest helped convince Louis's parents that he should enter this school and also helped arrange a scholarship for the boy.

On the morning of February 15, 1819, Louis said good-bye to his mother and then walked with his father to the stagecoach station. He couldn't know it at the time, but, except for periodic visits, he was never to make his home in Coupvray again. Four hours later Louis and his father arrived at their destination, the National Institute for the Young Blind on St. Victor Street in Paris. After speaking to several of the school's officials, Simon Braille parted from his ten-year-old son and returned to Coupvray.

The first few days, Louis wished he had never asked to go to the school. He couldn't find his way from his bunk to the bathroom or from the classroom to the dormitory, and often he either tripped or got lost. He had come from a very loving home, and he was upset by the antics of the other students, many of whom liked to fight in the dormitory and play tricks on one another. To make things worse, when the blind students were taken outside for walks, children would call them names and sometimes even throw things at them.

Slowly, however, Louis eased into the routine of the school. He learned to count the steps between his bed and the bathroom, and from the dormitory to the cafeteria. He made several friends among the students, and was soon exchanging jokes with them, helping them with their work, and even getting into occasional fights. But the best part about the school was the fact that his mind was greatly stimulated.

Not only was he being taught many subjects, including how to play the piano and the organ, for the first time in his life Louis was able to read. Valentin Haüy, the school's founder, had devised an ingenious reading method for his students. He had arranged for books with embossed, or raised, letters to be printed. By feeling the letters, the blind young people could make out the words.

First, Louis was taught to recognize the written alphabet and also the sounds that the letters made. Once he could do that, he began reading the books. Although people had read to Louis in the past, reading by himself was a wonderful new experience. He could pause to think about the author's words if he wanted, reread the best parts, and skip the boring parts.

Like many young people who have just begun to read, Louis Braille developed a hunger for books. Unfortunately, there was nothing for him to read once he'd finished the school's few embossed books. It was difficult to print the books by the Haüy method. Each letter had to be many times larger than the usual printed letter. Because of the large size of the letters, a book had to be divided into about twenty separate parts, each weighing about twenty pounds. This meant that a single book might weigh four hundred pounds! Another problem was that, despite the large size of the letters, it wasn't always easy for the students to tell an *h* from an *n*, or an *i* from an *l*. This made for very slow reading.

Louis's hunger for reading materials inspired him to think about better ways of creating books for the blind. Even at the age of eleven, it seemed to him that the key was to find a simple code for the letters. During the next several years he tried to think of ways that this could be done.

Louis began to work late every night, testing various methods for achieving his goal. He tried codes made of mathematical symbols and ones that used foreign words. During his vacations, Louis would return to Coupvray and go into his father's shop just as he'd done as a little boy. While Simon Braille worked away making saddles, Louis would cut shapes out of the leather and try to think of how shapes could be used to express letters.

Each method Louis thought of had drawbacks, however. Some were as complex as Haüy's letter-embossing method and would require huge volumes. With simpler methods it was often difficult to determine what the symbols were, meaning that the reader would have to spend a lot of time deciphering each word.

Just as Louis Braille was beginning to despair, he heard of a French army captain named Charles Barbier, who had invented a method for sending messages in the dark. Barbier's system, called "night writing," consisted of dots and dashes raised on paper. By touching the dots and dashes, the soldiers could decipher the message without using a light. Night after night, Louis Braille worked at creating a writing system for the blind based on dots and dashes. In 1824 he finally worked out the basics of what became the *braille system*. Louis Braille, whose method has since helped tens of thousands of blind people read, was only fifteen years old when he invented his system.

Like most new inventions, the braille system was not accepted at first. By this time, Valentin Haüy had died. The other officials at the school resented Braille's system. They had already spent a fortune producing books by the letter-embossing method, and they didn't want to have to learn how to teach a new method.

The fact that the other blind students were interested in his method buoyed Louis Braille's spirits. In 1826, when he was only seventeen, Braille became a teacher at the institute. Soon after this he eliminated the dashes from his system and transformed it into the dot system still used. This system is based on from one to six raised dots arranged in various patterns. By running their fingers over the dots, the blind readers made out the symbols for individual letters, various simple words, and several common speech sounds.

During the day, Louis taught the students by the old embossing method. But at night, he created his own handmade editions of Shakespeare's works and other classics, using his method. He used a pointed instrument similar to an awl to poke the raised dots into the paper. The students at the institute knew what Louis was doing, and some of them secretly came to his room at night to learn his method and read the books he had created. Many years later, an ex-pupil at the institute explained that school officials were so resentful of Louis Braille's reading method that, he said, "We had to learn [Braille's] alphabet in secret, and when we were caught using it, we were punished."

Louis Braille promoted his method for the rest of his life. He showed it to scholars of the day, but received little help from them. He even made friends with various wealthy people in Paris and demonstrated the braille method at parties they gave. People clapped and shouted, "Well done!" but nothing more came of it.

Although the world showed little interest in his invention, Louis Braille continued to teach it to all blind people who were interested. He also hired blind young people to translate books into braille. These books became his library, which he lent to other blind people.

Toward the end of Braille's life, several European countries began to notice and make use of his system. However, Louis Braille never saw his method achieve the great popularity it enjoys today. Having suffered from tuberculosis for many years, Braille died on January 6, 1852, just two days after his forty-third birthday. Ironically, at the time of his death Braille was better known as a musician than as the inventor of a reading system for the blind. An outstanding pianist and organist, he had served for many years as organist in a church close to the institute.

In the years following Louis Braille's death, more and more countries adopted his method. Today the braille system, named after him but sometimes spelled with a lowercase *b,* is the standard method for bringing the written word to the blind. Because of the invention of a fifteen-year-old boy, blind people today can read thousands of books. But Louis Braille did more than find a way for the blind to read. He demonstrated that, when given the opportunity, the blind can participate in the mainstream of life.

María de Sautuola

(1870–1946)

María de Sautuola lived with her family in a castle in the town of Santillana del Mar, which is in far northern Spain in the province of Santander. The family estate, Altamira (meaning "high view" in Spanish), was appropriately named. The region of Spain where María lived was filled with mountains, ridges, cliffs, and caves.

María's father, Don Marcelino de Sautuola, was quite interested in archaeology, which is the study of the remains of past human cultures. His interest grew stronger when he attended a Paris exhibition where prehistoric tools were displayed. Observing that many of the artifacts had been found in caves,

Don Marcelino wondered if there might be remains of prehistoric people in a cave located on his own property. This cave had been discovered several years before María's birth by a hunter whose dog had disappeared inside it.

In the late 1870s Don Marcelino began to explore and excavate his cave. It was lonely work, and so he began taking María with him for company. María would hold candles for her father, and sometimes she would help him dig. Together they found various tools, indicating that people had once lived in the cave, but not until one summer day in 1879 did they find anything spectacular.

On this day María accompanied her father to the cave on the hillside. At first she stayed quite close to her father, who was digging just a few feet from the entrance. Not far from the entrance there was a large hall, but Don Marcelino hadn't yet gotten around to excavating it and María hadn't gathered the courage to explore it on her own. Perhaps because she was bored on this particular day, María asked her father if she could enter the great hall. He gave his permission.

María took a candle and walked from the entrance into the large hall. She was standing inside and looking up at the eerie shapes that the candle cast on the ceiling when suddenly she noticed something that startled her. An eye was staring down at her. The next moment María realized that the eye belonged to an animal painted on the ceiling, and that there were more animals painted there.

"*Toros! Toros!*" the eight-year-old girl shouted, meaning "Bulls! Bulls!"

Wondering how bulls could have gotten inside his cave, Don Marcelino rushed into the great hall. When he looked up to see what María was staring at, Don Marcelino beheld more than a dozen of what María had called "*toros.*" Actually, they were bison — animals that María had never seen because they no longer existed in Spain. Don Marcelino observed that in all there were fifteen beautifully painted bison on the ceiling of the great hall, as well as three wild boars, three deer, two horses, and a wolf.

Despite the bright colors and amazingly realistic details in the paintings, Don Marcelino was convinced that they were many thousands of years old. For one thing, different styles were used, indicating that the paintings had been done over a long period of time. For another, it was unlikely that people had lived in the cave during modern times. A third proof was that the bison portrayed in the painting hadn't existed in Spain for more than ten thousand years.

Don Marcelino wrote letters to the leading archaeologists of the day about his daughter's discovery. One of them, Professor Juan de Vilanova y Piera of Madrid, came to the cave and studied the paintings. Professor Vilanova said that the paintings were thousands of years old and that María had made a great discovery.

Professor Vilanova helped Don Marcelino get in touch with newspapers and scientists. Journalists came and wrote stories about the "Cave of Altamira," as they called it, and about the girl and her father who had discovered the prehistoric art gallery. The scientists of the world, however, were silent. Not one of them besides Professor Vilanova would even come to the cave. In those days it was widely believed that prehistoric people had been club-wielding savages who had none of the "finer feelings" possessed by modern people. If they accepted the fact that artists of fifteen thousand years ago had created the lovely paintings in Don Marcelino's cave, the scientists would have to change their entire concept of prehistoric human beings. The scientists also said that the freshness of the paint suggested the pictures had been done recently. They even suspected that Don Marcelino had arranged to have the pictures painted in the cave so he could become famous.

Unfortunately, circumstances were against Don Marcelino. Wasn't it strange, people said, that this amateur archaeologist had made this discovery right on his own property? Another fact sealed the case for Don Marcelino's critics. It was revealed that a French artist had been working at the de Sautuola castle shortly before the discovery was made. The artist's job had been to restore some paintings in the castle. However, many people believed the artist had really been painting the "prehistoric" cave pictures.

In 1880 the world's archaeology professors held a conference at Lisbon, Portugal. Professor Vilanova tried to convince them of the authenticity of the paintings at the Cave of Altamira. He pointed out that the paintings had been done in so many styles that one person couldn't possibly have done them all. The professors didn't believe him and wouldn't visit the cave to see for themselves. That same year María's father published a pamphlet about the cave, but people dismissed it as the work of a "fake."

The newspapers now printed more stories about Don Marcelino and María. But instead of being hailed as discoverers, Don Marcelino was labeled a "fraud" and a "swindler," and María was portrayed as an innocent dupe. The articles claimed that María's father had expected her to stumble upon the faked paintings and had used her to promote their authenticity.

"If only they'd come see it for themselves, then they'd know that the paintings are genuine!" he'd say, as he read the articles.

María, now ten years old, was disappointed that she was no longer hailed as "The Girl of Altamira — discoverer of the prehistoric cave paintings." But it made her feel even worse to see her father suffering so badly. She could tell that it wasn't just a matter of science for him. His pride and sense of honor were deeply wounded by his being branded a liar.

Soon Don Marcelino didn't seem to care for food, sleep, or the other pleasant aspects of life. His way of dressing grew sloppy, his hair turned grayer by the week, and he often paced through the castle for hours or went out to the cave by himself.

During the next several years María did the things other wealthy young girls of her time did: she went to parties and balls and made many friends, including young men. To María, each passing year made the episode in the cave seem more like something out of the distant past. To her father, though, it had become an obsession. He continually wrote letters and often attended archaeological meetings in an effort to convince scientists to visit his cave. He was so obsessed by it that people began to consider him rather odd.

In 1888, when he was only fifty-seven, Don Marcelino became ill and died. María, now eighteen years old, felt that her father's sadness over the cave had hastened his death. From time to time, María told scientists about the cave, but with no success. When Professor Vilanova died in 1893, the cause seemed completely hopeless; he had been their link with the scientific community. But then several events changed everything.

What happened was that caves containing prehistoric art were found in France. Suddenly scientists became very interested in the Cave of Altamira. In 1902 several of them arranged with María de Sautuola to visit the cave.

On the day that the professors arrived, María, who by now was thirty-two years old and had her own family, led them to the hill. She unlocked the gate that had been placed in front of the cave following the death of her father. After handing the scientists lighted candles, María led them into the cave's great hall.

The professors stood there open-mouthed for a while, and then spent many minutes examining the paintings. When they finally spoke, they said such things as "Magnificent!" and "These are the greatest cave paintings yet discovered!" Then they told María that they were sorry for having doubted her father. In a letter to the author of this book, María de Sautuola's son, Emilio Botín, explained that for the rest of her life his mother was fond of telling the story about how the professors asked for forgiveness when she brought them into the cave in 1902.

Standing there with the professors, María could only wish that all this had occurred twenty years earlier, when her father would have appreciated it. After this visit, archaeologists and other scientists wrote papers and books apologizing to María and her dead father. "The Girl of Altamira" finally took her rightful place among the world's great discoverers.

Helen Keller

(1880–1968)

Five-year-old Helen Adams Keller knew that her mother was leaving the kitchen because she could feel the vibrations of her footsteps on the floor. The little girl, who was completely blind and deaf, grabbed her mother's skirt and followed her to the pantry. Not wanting to enter the small, hot room, Helen waited outside while Mrs. Keller went in to get some canned goods.

Helen didn't know that the little room she was standing near was called the "pantry," nor did she know that this woman who took care of her was called "Mother." Helen had been cut off from the world of sight and sound for more than three years.

At the age of nineteen months she had become ill with a high fever, and the illness had destroyed her eyesight and hearing.

As Helen waited for her mother, she felt a metal object sticking out of a hole in the pantry door. She discovered that when she twisted this metal object a certain way, the door could not be opened. Several times Helen locked and unlocked the door. Finally she left the door locked and then went outside and sat down on the porch steps.

A short while later Mrs. Keller finished her work in the pantry and tried to open the door. Helen could feel the vibrations of her mother's furious pounding on the door, but the little girl just sat there giggling to herself. The harder her mother pounded, the harder Helen laughed. Finally a servant in a distant wing of the house heard Mrs. Keller's pounding and came to let her out.

As usual, Helen went unpunished for her misbehavior. Her parents, Kate and Arthur Keller, could not bear to discipline her. This latest prank, however, reminded the Kellers of something they had recently discussed. They had to find a way to teach Helen the basics of civilized behavior.

Although the Kellers had already taken Helen to numerous doctors, they decided to take her to a famous eye specialist in Baltimore before giving up completely on her eyesight. Shortly after the pantry incident, Helen and her family went by train from their home in Tuscumbia, Alabama, to Baltimore, Maryland. The eye specialist said that nothing could be done to restore Helen's sight, but he added that there was a scientist in Washington, D.C., who would know how Helen could be educated.

From Baltimore the Kellers made the short trip to Washington, where they visited this scientist, who was the famous Alexander Graham Bell. Although Bell is best known for inventing the telephone, he spent much of his life working with the deaf. After the Kellers were shown into Bell's office, Helen sat right down on the big man's knees. Bell gave Helen his watch to play with and observed her for a while. Then he explained to her parents that Helen was extremely intelligent and that she was mischievous because she was frustrated about not being able to communicate.

Bell then advised the Kellers to write to the Perkins Institution for the Blind in Boston because he thought that this school could provide a teacher for Helen. When they returned to Tuscumbia, Helen's father wrote to Perkins, and several weeks later he received word that a teacher for Helen had been found.

The teacher, Anne Sullivan, arrived by train at Tuscumbia on March 3, 1887, four months before Helen's seventh birthday. During Anne's childhood in Massachusetts, her mother had died, and she had been abandoned by her father. Anne had

grown up in a state institution for the impoverished — the "poorhouse," as it was commonly
called — and there she had lost nearly all of her
sight. Fortunately, when she was fourteen, Anne
had left the poorhouse and entered the Perkins
Institution, where she had learned to read in braille.
The school had also arranged for her to undergo
several operations in Boston, which had partially
restored her sight. On the spring day when Anne
Sullivan stepped off the train in Tuscumbia, she
was only twenty years old.

Many years later, in her autobiography, *The
Story of My Life,* Helen Keller wrote about her first
encounter with Anne Sullivan:

> I felt approaching footsteps. I stretched out
> my hand as I supposed to my mother. Some
> one took it, and I was caught up and held
> close in the arms of her who had come to
> reveal all things to me, and, more than all
> things else, to love me.

Helen ran her hands over Miss Sullivan's face,
clothes, and traveling bag. When her mother pulled
her away from the bag, Helen went into one of her
tantrums. The little girl wouldn't quiet down until
Miss Sullivan allowed her to hold her wristwatch.

The next morning as Miss Sullivan unpacked,
Helen entered the young woman's room and began

rummaging through her traveling bag. When she discovered a doll in the bag, the little girl pointed to herself in a questioning way. Miss Sullivan placed Helen's hand on her head and nodded so that Helen would know that the answer was "yes." Then, holding Helen's hand, Miss Sullivan spelled out "d-o-l-l" several times in the girl's palm, using the special manual alphabet employed by people who can't talk. Helen then took Miss Sullivan's hand and spelled out "d-o-l" (she had trouble with the second *l* at first) on her palm. Helen was so excited about doing this that she ran downstairs and spelled out "d-o-l" in her mother's hand.

Miss Sullivan now went down to the kitchen to get a big piece of cake. She let Helen smell and touch the cake, but she wouldn't let her eat it until she spelled "c-a-k-e." Helen began to yell and kick, but quieted down when she realized she wouldn't get the cake without spelling it. Anne Sullivan spelled "c-a-k-e" into Helen's palm again. When Helen finally spelled it back to her, she was given the treat.

During the next several days Helen learned to write "p-i-n," "h-a-t," "c-u-p," "s-i-t," "w-a-l-k," and several other words in the manual alphabet. Helen liked all the attention Miss Sullivan was giving her, but the little girl often felt angry at her, too. No matter how big a tantrum Helen threw, the woman would not give her cake or sweets until after she had spelled the words for the day. Besides, the woman was forever trying to get Helen to eat with some weird metal objects and a strange kind of cloth in her lap.

One morning at breakfast, after Anne Sullivan had been with the Kellers for four days, Helen dipped her fingers into her own as well as everyone else's plate as usual. Her mother and father didn't mind when Helen grabbed their pancakes, but when the little girl took Miss Sullivan's the teacher grabbed them back. When Helen began screaming and kicking at her, Miss Sullivan shoved the little girl back into her chair and asked her parents to leave the room.

For more than a half hour Helen and her teacher fought and wrestled as Miss Sullivan tried to force the girl to eat off her own plate and to use silverware and a napkin. When Helen finally submitted to her teacher's will, both of them were smeared with syrup and there were pancakes and silverware all over the floor. That night Anne Sullivan wrote a letter to a friend describing this fight:

> I had a battle royal with Helen this morning. . . . Then [after the fight] I let her out into the warm sunshine and went up to my room and threw myself on the bed exhausted. I had a good cry and felt better. I suppose I shall have many such battles with the little

woman before she learns the only two essential things I can teach her, obedience and love.

Although Miss Sullivan did have "many such battles" with Helen at the beginning, the girl gradually began to follow her instructions. Helen could tell that the teacher liked her very much and she wanted to please the woman. Besides, Helen found that she liked doing things the way everyone else did. For example, although she couldn't understand the sense of eating with the metal objects instead of with her hands, she felt less cut off from other people when she ate like them.

After a few days at the Keller house, Anne Sullivan obtained permission to live alone with Helen for a time at the "garden house" several blocks from the Keller home. There, undisturbed by Helen's parents, the little girl and her teacher studied and ate together and even slept in the same bed. During their two weeks at the cottage Helen learned more words and also learned to trust and obey her teacher completely.

Helen couldn't know this, but something was bothering Miss Sullivan about the little girl's use of words. Helen did not seem to understand that words corresponded to objects and ideas. For example, when Helen wanted cake she would write out "c-a-k-e" in the manual alphabet. But as far as she was concerned this was just a code for getting what she wanted. She did not understand that the word "c-a-k-e" actually stands for the object we call a cake. Helen herself later wrote in her autobiography:

> I did not know that I was spelling a word or even that words existed; I was simply making my fingers go in monkey-like imitation.

Anne Sullivan continued to spell words into Helen's hand, hoping that she would realize the true nature of words. But when the time came for the two of them to return to the main house, the breakthrough was still several weeks away.

On the morning of April 5, 1887, Helen was washing her face when she asked Miss Sullivan the "code" for water. Miss Sullivan spelled "w-a-t-e-r" into her hand. After breakfast, when Helen and Miss Sullivan were out in the garden, they went to the pump for a drink of water. As the cold liquid flowed into the little girl's mug, Miss Sullivan again wrote "w-a-t-e-r" into Helen's free hand. Suddenly Helen dropped her mug and stood with a startled look on her face as the water poured over her hand. Before her illness, Helen had known several words, including "wah-wah" — her way of saying "water." Now as her teacher spelled out "w-a-t-e-r" in her hand, Helen realized that this was the specific word for this substance. Years later, Helen Keller recalled this wondrous moment in her autobiography:

> As the cool stream gushed over one hand she spelled into the other the word *water,* first slowly, then rapidly. I stood still, my whole attention fixed upon the motions of her fingers. Suddenly I felt a misty consciousness as of something forgotten — a thrill of returning thought; and somehow the mystery of language was revealed to me. I knew then that "w-a-t-e-r" meant the wonderful cool something that was flowing over my hand. That living word awakened my soul, gave it light, hope, joy, set it free!

Helen excitedly pointed to the ground, the pump, the flower trellis, and her baby sister, and asked Miss Sullivan to tell her what they all were called. The teacher told Helen the names of these things and then the girl pointed to Miss Sullivan herself. Miss Sullivan spelled "t-e-a-c-h-e-r" into Helen's hand, and from then on that is what Helen called her.

Now that she understood the nature of words, Helen wanted to know what everything was called. Miss Sullivan taught her the names of the flowers, birds, and other objects they encountered in their daily lives. By the time Helen had learned a few dozen words, Miss Sullivan decided to communicate with her in complete sentences without pausing to define every new word. This method worked beautifully. Helen figured out the meaning of words from the way they were used, and soon the six-year-old girl was expressing herself in whole sentences.

Deciding that Helen was now ready to learn how to read, Anne Sullivan obtained a few simple storybooks and read them to the little girl in the manual alphabet. Several of the books had raised letters. After Miss Sullivan taught Helen how to identify the letters, Helen began reading by herself. Helen liked reading so much that she sometimes took books to bed with her and read them in the dark. When Miss Sullivan told Helen that she shouldn't take her books to bed, the little girl wrote this explanation on her teacher's palm: "Helen is not afraid. Book is afraid. Book will sleep with girl." Teacher then explained that, even though the book was afraid, it had to go to sleep in the bookcase.

In the summer of 1887, when Helen was barely seven, Miss Sullivan taught her braille — the method of writing letters using small raised dots. Helen learned it rapidly, and soon she was reading books printed in braille and using the system to correspond with people.

When Helen was still seven years old, she and Miss Sullivan were invited to the Perkins Institution in Boston. Helen was so excited about the upcoming trip that she wrote this letter to the Institution's blind children:

> Helen will write little blind girls a letter   Helen and teacher will come to see little blind girls Helen and teacher will go in steam car to boston   Helen and blind girls will have fun blind girls can talk on fingers   . . . Helen will go to school with blind girls   Helen can read and count and spell and write like blind girls . . . papa does shoot ducks with gun and ducks do fall in water and jumbo and mamie do swim in water and bring ducks out in mouth to papa   Helen does play with dogs   Helen does ride on horseback with teacher . . . Helen is blind   Helen will put letter in envelope for blind girls
>
> good-by
> Helen Keller

In May 1888 Helen and her teacher took the train to Boston. That spring Helen spent several months studying literature, arithmetic, and other subjects with the blind children at Perkins, while also continuing her lessons with Miss Sullivan.

During the next several years Helen and her teacher spent much of their time at Perkins. Helen had a particular passion for literature, and by the time she was nine she had read such books as *Little Women, Robinson Crusoe,* Charles and Mary Lamb's

Tales from Shakespeare, and various fables and Bible stories. By that time Helen had also learned some French, German, Latin, and Greek, and often quoted from these languages in her daily "conversations," using the manual alphabet.

When Helen was nine, one of the teachers at Perkins told her about a blind and deaf Norwegian girl who had learned to speak by touching people's lips as they spoke and memorizing the shapes of the letters. Helen became very excited about this and wrote into her teacher's palm: "I want to learn to speak."

Miss Sullivan took Helen to Miss Sarah Fuller, principal of Boston's Horace Mann School for the Deaf. In the spring of 1890 Miss Fuller gave Helen eleven lessons. By the time the lessons were over Helen could put sounds together well enough to speak in a barely intelligible manner.

Because newspapers and magazines printed stories about the blind and deaf girl who had learned so much in so short a time, Helen had become quite well known by her tenth birthday in the summer of 1890. Several years later, Helen attended a college preparatory school for a while with her teacher at her side to translate the lessons for her. Helen then enrolled at Radcliffe College. Before graduating from Radcliffe with honors in 1904, Helen Keller wrote *The Story of My Life,* in which she related how Anne Sullivan had transformed her from an angry child into the best-educated blind and deaf person in the world.

As an adult, Helen Keller dedicated her life to helping handicapped people. She lectured, wrote books, gave speeches before lawmakers, and also raised money on behalf of the handicapped. One of her most important contributions to the blind concerned the braille system. By the early 1900s there were several separate braille systems in use, which caused much confusion. In 1932 Helen Keller helped get a single braille system adopted as the official reading system for the blind. The particular method adopted was very close to the exact system that Louis Braille had invented a century earlier.

Anne Sullivan and Helen Keller lived together for forty-nine years until Miss Sullivan's death in 1936 at the age of seventy. Helen Keller outlived her teacher by many years and died in 1968 at the age of eighty-eight.

Pablo Picasso

(1881–1973)

Eight-year-old Pablo Picasso often came to school with his sketchbook and pencils in one hand and a fluttering pigeon in the other. While the other students did their geography or their reading lesson, Pablo would raise up the lid of his desk to protect him from the view of his classmates. Then he would make sketches of the pigeon. Sometimes he would get out of his seat and go to the window, or leave the room entirely and walk around the school. The teacher did not criticize Pablo for his odd behavior, and the children did not laugh at it.

This school, the Colegio San Rafaelo, was the second school Pablo had attended in his hometown of Málaga, which lies along the Mediterranean Sea on Spain's southern coast. Several years earlier Pablo's parents had enrolled him in a public school, but the boy's career there had been a disaster. The teachers and the principal had expected Pablo to stay in his seat and hadn't liked it when he sketched during the lessons. The Colegio San Rafaelo was much better for Pablo. It was a private school and the principal was a family friend. No one here minded when Pablo sketched during the lessons or even wandered out of the classroom.

After finishing each sketch, Pablo would sign it. He liked writing his name — which in full was Pablo Diego José Francisco de Paula Juan Nepomuceno María de los Remedios Cipriano de la Santísima Trinidad Ruiz Picasso — in various ways. Sometimes he signed his name "P. Ruiz," while other times he wrote it "P. Picasso," "P. Ruiz Picasso," "P. R. Picasso," or just "Picasso."

Pablo realized that it was important for him to learn to count and read a little, so on every day that he attended school he tried to concentrate on the lessons for at least a short while. He had trouble doing this, however, because everything reminded him of art. During the arithmetic lesson the zeros would remind him of eyes, and the threes would make him think of birds' wings. Soon Pablo would give up trying to concentrate, flip open his sketchbook, and begin another drawing.

There was one time that Pablo could recognize on the clock: 1:00, the hour when school ended. As soon as the teacher dismissed the students Pablo would go outside to meet his father. In fact, he would only go to school if he could take along his father's brushes or one of his pigeons, and if his father would promise to meet him at dismissal time. Every day when Pablo's father picked him up from school he would ask the boy what he had learned, and every day the story was much the same — many drawings but no schoolwork.

Art had been the main thing in Pablo's life for as long as the boy could remember. Pablo's father, Don José Ruiz, was the curator of the municipal art museum in Málaga. There Don José spent his days touching up the museum's old paintings. Don José also had his own studio at the museum, where he painted realistic pictures of landscapes, flowers, and pigeons. These he occasionally sold to augment the family's income.

As soon as Pablo had learned to walk, his father had taken him along to the museum. There Pablo had watched in fascination as his father restored old paintings and created his own new ones. Don José had shown his eager son how to draw with pencils, charcoal, crayons, and watercolors, and had also taught him about color values, perspective, and composition.

Quite early Pablo had shown that he was extremely talented, and that he had a one-track mind about art, much like young Mozart's about music. The drawings Picasso made even at the age of eight were remarkably mature. In fact, visitors to the family's apartment found it difficult to believe that a child had drawn the pictures of bullfights and pigeons that were fastened all over the walls.

Now that Pablo was eight years old he wanted to do oil paintings, like his father. He asked his father about it, and Don José presented his eager son with a canvas, then showed him how to prepare it and mix the paints.

For the first painting Pablo decided to portray a bullfighter on horseback. Pablo's five-year-old sister, Lola, watched as he painted the horse, the bull-fighter in a yellow jacket, and three people in the stands. The painting had amazing harmony and warmth for the work of an eight-year-old, but there was something about it Lola didn't like. Pablo hadn't painted in the eyes of the three people in the stands. Pablo's little sister remedied this situation by taking a nail and poking holes in the canvas where she thought the eyes should be! For the rest of his life there were to be many people who, like Lola, complained that Pablo didn't portray things as they really looked.

When he was eight or nine years old, Pablo created a number of very fine oil paintings. His subjects were biblical scenes, his sister Lola, and the people he met on the streets of Málaga. Because Pablo Picasso grew up to become one of the most famous artists who ever lived, many of these early works are housed in museums today and are worth thousands of dollars.

When Pablo was ten, a big change took place in his life. The museum where Pablo's father was curator was closed, and so Don José found himself without a job. He finally located a teaching position at the School of Fine Arts in La Coruña, a city seven hundred miles from Málaga on Spain's northwestern coast. The family left their home in sunny southern Spain, and sailed to the country's rainy and foggy northwestern shore.

La Coruña was a picturesque port city, and Pablo found the change interesting. He attended classes, including those taught by his father, at the School of Fine Arts. Pablo improved so rapidly that by the time he was thirteen the sketches and paintings he was continually creating looked like the work of a very talented adult. One of his paintings at this time was *Girl with Bare Feet,* which showed a sad, sullen girl in a red dress. Pablo liked this painting so much that he kept it with him wherever he lived for the rest of his life.

Don José disliked La Coruña as much as Pablo liked it. He spent much of his time staring out the window at the rain instead of painting. Pablo later told biographers that his father had come to the bittersweet realization that he was only a mediocre artist and that the greatest contribution he could make would be to encourage his very talented son. One day when Pablo was thirteen, his father decided to give up painting altogether. Decades later, when recalling this incident, Pablo Picasso said: "He then gave me his paints and brushes, and never painted again."

Just before Pablo's fourteenth birthday his family moved again — this time to Barcelona, a large city in northeastern Spain, where Don José had obtained a teaching position at the School of Fine Arts. When he enrolled at this school, Pablo found that he was about five years younger than the youngest of its more than one hundred students. Pablo's parents rented a tiny studio for him just around the corner from the family's apartment. After a full day of studying art at the school, Pablo would go to his studio to paint. Sometimes he would spend the entire night there, painting and discussing art with his classmates.

One day in 1896 Don José told Pablo that if he wanted to become a professional artist it would be good for him to win some awards. In 1896 and 1897 Pablo painted three large works, which had been methodically planned out by father and son. The paintings were the kind of pleasant, realistic works that were popular with the general public and the critics at that time. Two of the paintings —

The Choir Boy and *First Communion* — depicted religious subjects. The third — *Science and Charity* — portrayed a doctor and his patient.

Science and Charity won two awards: an honorable mention at the Madrid General Fine Arts Exhibition and a gold medal at the Provincial Exhibition in Málaga, Pablo's birthplace. Critics praised the work, and many predicted a bright future for the fifteen-year-old artist.

Pablo did have a bright future, but he followed a much different path from the one people expected. As an adult, he decided that he would portray things the way he thought and felt about them rather than in the traditional realistic manner. During one period of Picasso's life, called his "Blue Period," many of his paintings were composed with blue as the predominant color. After that, Picasso helped develop the art movements called *cubism* (in which objects are portrayed in the form of cubes and other basic geometric shapes) and *collage* (in which artists incorporate such objects as newspaper clippings and pieces of debris into their works).

At first many people thought that Pablo had lost his mind when they saw that he had depicted people in the shape of rectangles and had pasted newspaper clippings onto his paintings. But eventually Picasso was hailed for his innovative and interesting approach to art. Not only was the quality of Picasso's work outstanding, he probably produced more work than any artist who has ever lived. Picasso never stopped creating, and by the time he died at the age of ninety-one he had produced more than fifteen thousand paintings, tens of thousands of drawings, and many pieces of sculpture and ceramics. Today Pablo Picasso is remembered as one of the greatest artists of the twentieth century.

Hilda Conkling

(1910–1986)

Six-year-old Hilda Conkling and her mother had a bedtime ritual. Almost every night Mrs. Conkling would sit on the edge of Hilda's bed and read to her from a book of poetry or stories. Sometimes, when her mother closed the book, Hilda would say, "I have a poem for you, Mother." Then Hilda would recite the poem that she had composed in her mind.

Mrs. Conkling always had a pencil and paper ready so that she could write down Hilda's poems. The little girl thought that perhaps her mother placed the poems in a scrapbook or something like that. Had she known her mother's true intentions, she would have been very surprised.

The three Conklings — Hilda, her older sister, Elsa, and their mother, Grace Hazard Conkling — lived in Northampton, a town of about twenty thousand people, in western Massachusetts. Hilda's parents had separated shortly after her birth, but Mrs. Conkling tried to make up for being the sole parent in the house by spending a great deal of time with her daughters. The three of them went for daily walks in the woods near their house. The Conklings also participated in artistic activities together. The family loved music, and on many evenings Mrs. Conkling would play the piano while Elsa played the violin and Hilda listened. In addition, the three of them often discussed music and painting. At the heart of their life together, however, was poetry.

Mrs. Conkling, who taught literature at Smith College, just up the hill from their house, was a widely published poet. For several hours each day, she sat in her chair and worked on her poems while the girls sat nearby and read. Even the family's best friends were poets. Hilda often listened as her mother discussed rhythm, imagery, and melody with Robert Frost, Amy Lowell, and other famous poets who visited the house. In the evening, Mrs. Conkling and the girls often entertained themselves by attending poetry readings and lectures at Smith College.

Hilda, a very shy girl, flourished in this quiet, creative environment. She had few friends and had little to do with anyone except her mother and Elsa. When she was alone, Hilda liked to read, look at the garden, or just sit and daydream. The smell of the spring wind, the sound of leaves being blown off trees in the autumn, the sight of a spider's web glistening in the sun: these were the sorts of things that gave Hilda joy and inspired her to compose poems.

Ever since she had composed her first poems at the age of four, Hilda had always told her mother about a new poem in their special bedtime ritual. All the observations she made while walking around Northampton or sitting and daydreaming came to life in Hilda's poems. Here are two poems Hilda composed by the time she was eight:

WATER
The world turns softly
Not to spill its lakes and rivers.
The water is held in its arms
And the sky is held in the water.
What is water,
That pours silver,
And can hold the sky?

SILVERHORN
It is out in the mountains
I find him,
My snowy deer

With silver horns like dew,
Horns that sparkle.
I think I see him in the hollow,
He is on the high hill!
I think I see him on the hill,
He is leaping through the air!
I think I can ride upon his back,
He is like moonlight I cannot hold,
He is like thoughts I lose.
He flows by
All white . . .
He makes me think of the brook
Out of the hills
With its little foamy points
Like his twitching ears,
Like his horns of silver
Sparkling.

The brook is his only friend
When he travels . . .
Silverhorn, Silverhorn!

When Hilda was eight, Mrs. Conkling decided that there were enough good poems to begin sending groups of them to various publications. Without telling Hilda, Mrs. Conkling mailed off some of her little girl's work to such adult magazines as *Poetry, Good Housekeeping, The Delineator,* and *Contemporary Verse.* The editors liked the poems and, beginning in 1919, published quite a few of them.

It was an amazing accomplishment for a nine-year-old to be published in those magazines, especially *Poetry,* which was one of the most prestigious literary publications in the world. Hilda didn't get to enjoy her achievement, however, because her mother hid the magazines. Mrs. Conkling explained to interviewers that she did this out of fear that Hilda might become self-conscious and lose some of her creativity if she saw her poems in print.

About the time of Hilda's ninth birthday, in 1919, Mrs. Conkling gathered more than a hundred of the little girl's poems and secretly sent them to the Frederick A. Stokes Company, a New York publisher. The editors at Stokes loved the poems and in 1920 they published them in a book called *Poems by a Little Girl.* In the preface to the book Amy Lowell wrote: "I know of no other instance in which such really beautiful poetry has been written by a child," adding that Hilda possessed "that flash of personality which we call genius."

Critics at magazines were also referring to Hilda as a young "genius," interviewers were regularly phoning to find out about the little girl, and a movie producer wanted to make a newsreel about her. Realizing that she could no longer keep Hilda's accomplishments a secret from the child, Mrs. Conkling decided to give a surprise party for her younger daughter to celebrate her debut as an author.

On the day of the party Hilda came home to

find her mother, her sister, and a small group of her schoolmates sitting around the living room table. The table was filled with cake and ice cream, and on one of the plates there was a book with a pretty blue cover.

Hilda picked up the book and saw that it was entitled *Poems by a Little Girl* and that "Hilda Conkling" was listed below the title as the author. She opened the book and saw the first poem:

FOR YOU, MOTHER
I have a dream for you, Mother,
Like a soft thick fringe to hide your eyes.
I have a surprise for you, Mother,
Shaped like a strange butterfly.
I have found a way of thinking
To make you happy;
I have made a song and a poem
All twisted into one.
If I sing, you listen;
If I think, you know.
I have a secret from everybody in the world full of people
But I cannot always remember how it goes;
It is a song
For you, Mother,
With a curl of cloud and a feather of blue
And a mist
Blowing along the sky.
If I sing it some day, under my voice,
Will it make you happy?

Although Hilda was extremely bright (it was later determined that her I.Q. was 186), she was confused about something as she thanked her mother for the book. Hilda didn't realize that thousands of copies of the book had been printed and thought that her mother had somehow gotten the publisher to print just one copy as a present! This idea was soon dispelled when the Conklings were invited to a school in Vermont, where Hilda had to sign five hundred copies of her book. And when a film crew arrived at the Conkling house to make the newsreel about her, Hilda realized that she had even become something of a celebrity.

As soon as the excitement of her first book diminished a bit, Hilda resumed her evening poetry recitations to her mother. By the time she was ten, Hilda's powers of observation and vocabulary had grown quite sophisticated, as seen in the following poem:

BULBS
Bulbs in brown capes
As though they were dead . . .
As though they would never come alive!

But their life is real
Though you cannot see it:
White ribbons reach from them far and
  wide

Into mysterious water:
When you have given up all hope . . .
(How can you know their narcissus
*   thoughts?)*
They soften and rouse
And poke out green finger-tips.

Now Hilda was creating poem after poem with exquisite images. For example, in "Pigeons Just Awake" she said that the pigeons' "feet were the color of new June strawberries." In "Hill Song" she spoke of a brook containing "trout that wear coral beads."

As she had done before, Mrs. Conkling saved the poems Hilda composed when she was ten and eleven and sent them to magazines, where many more of them were published. Then Mrs. Conkling gathered up all the poems Hilda had created since *Poems by a Little Girl* was published and mailed them to the Stokes Company in New York. Stokes accepted the poems and in 1922 Hilda's second book, *Shoes of the Wind,* was published, also to great acclaim. Editors of other book companies also liked Hilda's work, and soon her poems were appearing in anthologies, alongside the work of such famous poets as Robert Frost and Walt Whitman.

Because Hilda Conkling was such a fine poet at twelve, many people expected her to become a great poet as an adult. This unfortunately did not happen. By the time she reached her teens, she was writing her poems instead of saying them to her mother, but the poems weren't coming as often as before. Her last book, *Silverhorn,* appeared when she was fourteen, but instead of containing new poems it merely reprinted ones from Hilda's first two books. By the time Hilda was twenty, her poems appeared only rarely in magazines.

As an adult, Hilda Conkling did social work with teenagers, worked in factories, operated bookshops, and was employed as a housekeeper. Although she still wrote an occasional poem, even people who knew her well didn't know that she had once been called a "genius" at the age of nine by Amy Lowell.

Sixty-four years after her first book was published, Hilda Conkling looked back on her years as a child poet and wrote the following in a letter to the author of this book:

> Even today, this whole thing is like talking about someone else. I look at the poems in astonishment that I could have said those things and their effect on others comes as a humble surprise. They have brought comfort as well as pleasure to many and if I do nothing more I am glad to have contributed something that makes having lived worthwhile.

Judy Garland

(1922–1969)

As she sat on her grandmother's lap and watched her two older sisters sing a duet on the stage of her family's movie theater, little Frances Gumm was unhappy. Everyone in the Gumm family except Frances got to perform. Mrs. Gumm played the piano while the movies — which were silent in those days — were shown. Between movies her parents, or her sisters, or all four of them, would go up onto the stage to sing. During all this the only thing two-and-a-half-year-old Frances was allowed to do was sit quietly and watch.

    On this particular evening, which was around Christmastime in 1924, Frances decided that she'd had enough of sitting quietly. She waited until the audience began clapping and then suddenly broke away from her grandmother and climbed onto the stage.

As Frances stood there looking out at the laughing faces, she didn't quite know what to do. Her mother, who was sitting at the piano beneath the stage, whispered loudly: "Get off, Baby, get off!" Frances didn't want to get off, however. Realizing that she couldn't just stand there, Frances began singing "Jingle Bells."

When Frances finished the song and the audience began to cheer, she bowed and giggled. "Okay, Baby, come on down!" her mother called, with a forced smile. Aware that she had received louder cheers than the rest of her family usually earned, and that her mother wasn't very angry with her, Frances sang "Jingle Bells" a second, and then a third, time. She thrust out her hands while she sang, and these gestures sometimes caused her to fall. When that happened, she just popped back up again in the funny way she had seen Charlie Chaplin do in the movies, and this brought even louder laughter and applause. Frances had sung "Jingle Bells" at least half a dozen times when finally her father marched up the aisle, came onto the stage, and picked her up.

"I want to sing more!" she yelled, as her father

carried her down the aisle past the roaring audience.

After this, Frances's parents and her sisters, Mary Jane and Virginia, taught her the family's musical repertoire and added her to the act. People who came to the New Grand Theater loved listening to "Little Miss Leather Lungs," as she was billed in advertisements, and Frances loved performing with her family for them.

The Gumm family lived in a lovely two-story house at 403 Second Avenue in Grand Rapids, a Minnesota papermilling town of about three thousand people. As the youngest — and also because she had nearly died several times in her infancy from an intestinal disorder — "Baby," as Frances was called, was treated like the queen of the household. All her life she was to remember her early childhood in Minnesota as an idyllic time of swimming, ice skating, having snowball fights, and performing with her family.

In summer of 1926 the Gumm family arranged for a neighbor to take care of their dog; then they set out on a California vacation. At the time, vaudeville, a form of live entertainment that featured a wide variety of theatrical acts, was extremely popular. As the Gumms headed west they stopped at vaudeville theaters where Mr. and Mrs. Gumm often managed to get their girls hired. In fact, Frances and her two sisters earned enough money in this way to pay for almost the entire vacation.

Mr. and Mrs. Gumm liked California so much that they decided to move the family there. In fall of 1926 the Gumms sold the New Grand Theater and the white frame house at 403 Second Avenue. Frances said good-bye to her friends and relatives, and then on a late-October morning she boarded a train with her mother and sisters and began the two-thousand-mile trip to California, with her father following in the family car.

Once they arrived in Los Angeles, the Gumms rented a house. While Mr. Gumm looked for a movie theater to operate, the girls brought in some money for the family by performing at various vaudeville halls, nightclubs, and hotels in the Los Angeles area. After several months, Mr. Gumm took over a movie theater in Lancaster, a town of about fifteen hundred people seventy miles northeast of Los Angeles. By the fall of 1927, Frances was enrolled in kindergarten at a school near her home in Lancaster, and she and her sisters were singing and dancing between movies at their father's Valley Theatre.

From time to time the Gumms drove to Los Angeles, where they sometimes visited Hollywood, the moviemaking section of the city. In Hollywood, Frances and her family visited various studios and watched such stars as Lillian Gish, Lon Chaney,

Marion Davies, and John Gilbert at work. In October 1927 the big news in Hollywood was that *The Jazz Singer* had just ushered in the age of "talking movies." When Mrs. Gumm learned that studios were searching for young actors and actresses who could speak clearly and sing well, she began to think that her girls might become movie stars.

Now when Mrs. Gumm took her daughters to Los Angeles for weekend nightclub engagements, it was with the hope that they would be noticed by movie executives. Very soon the girls were booked to appear on several of the city's radio stations, where they sang such songs as "You're the Cream in My Coffee" and "Avalon." They also landed minor singing roles in several short films, which the studios were cranking out by the hundreds in those days to accompany their main features.

By the time Frances turned seven everyone could see that she was the most talented of the three Gumm sisters. In fact, when the little girl with the large brown eyes sang a solo, people were surprised to hear such an expressive and mature voice coming out of such a little girl. Although the girls continued to perform together at the movie theater in Lancaster and at some other engagements, Mrs. Gumm began taking Frances alone to Los Angeles to audition for movie producers and agents, and to cities throughout southern California, where Frances obtained singing jobs.

Although Frances always made a big hit, she did not like singing alone. The applause did not make up for the loneliness she felt at being separated so often from her sisters and father. Another thing that bothered her was all the arguing her parents did in those days. Frances sensed that one reason for the weekend travel was that her mother wanted to get away from home as much as possible.

In the summer of 1934 Mrs. Gumm drove the girls all the way to Chicago, where she obtained a singing job for them at a café. Unfortunately, they weren't paid, because the café was controlled by gangsters. Mrs. Gumm then took the girls around to various Chicago theaters and nightclubs and finally landed a job for them at the Oriental Theater, where George Jessel's was the headline act. When they approached the Oriental on the night of their first performance, Frances, her sisters, and their mother eagerly looked up at the marquee. But instead of THE GUMM SISTERS, the marquee read THE GLUM SISTERS.

The three girls, particularly Frances, were a big hit at the Oriental. After the first show, George Jessel told Mrs. Gumm that he'd never before heard a child with a voice as good as Frances's. "But, Mrs. Gumm," he added, "I can't go out and keep introducing your girls as the Gumm Sisters. It gets a laugh, and you're not a comedy act. You've got to change your name." That same night Jessel came up with the last name of Garland for the three sisters. He is thought to have named them after Robert Garland, a New York theater critic.

Twelve-year-old Frances liked her new stage name, but she didn't think that Frances Garland sounded right. Since one of her favorite songs was entitled "Judy," she decided to adopt that as her first name. Upon their return to California she announced to her family that she no longer wanted to be called "Frances" or "Baby." From now on her name was Judy Garland.

During the summer of 1935, the Garland Sisters performed in a lodge at Lake Tahoe at the California–Nevada border. Several movie people heard Judy sing there, and one of them, an agent, said that he thought he could line up some work for Judy and that Mrs. Gumm should phone him.

Mrs. Gumm did call the agent, who arranged several auditions for Judy at movie studios. Although the executives at the studios thought that Judy sang beautifully, all of them felt that she was too overweight and not pretty enough to be star material.

By this time Judy's father was operating a theater in a small town just outside Los Angeles, and the family was living in Hollywood. One September afternoon, Judy was out in the yard tossing a ball to her wirehaired terrier, Waffles, when the agent called to say he'd lined up an audition for her at

Metro-Goldwyn-Mayer. Judy's mother usually took care of auditions, but she was in Pasadena on a piano-playing engagement. Judy's father went out into the yard and told her, "We're going to audition at Metro. Let's go."

"Daddy, I can't go like this; I'm a mess," said Judy, who was wearing a rumpled blouse, grass-stained slacks, and sneakers.

Mr. Gumm looked his daughter over and then said, "Come on. They'll like you as you are."

At the M-G-M studio, Judy sang a new song called "Zing Went the Strings of My Heart" for several officials. They were so impressed that the head of the studio was called in to listen. When Judy finished singing, the chief said, "Very nice, thank you very much," and left the room without a handshake or even a smile.

Judy's father, annoyed at the man's impoliteness, said, "Let's get out of here, Babe." The two of them drove home thinking the whole trip had just been a waste of time.

A few days later, however, the studio phoned and offered Judy a seven-year contract starting at $150 a week. The studio chief hadn't wanted to praise Judy's singing for fear that she might ask for more money. As it was, $150 per week was much more than most adults were earning in those years, and the family agreed to the terms. Because Judy was only thirteen years old, her mother had to sign the contract for her.

On an October day in 1935, Judy came through the M-G-M gates for the first time as an employee. With its two hundred acres, more than three thousand employees, and even its own police force, fire station, hospital, and school, the studio was like a little city. Judy was excited to be a part of this famous studio, and she was thrilled to find herself eating lunch at the M-G-M cafeteria alongside such stars as Joan Crawford, Clark Gable, Spencer Tracy, Greta Garbo, James Stewart, Mickey Rooney, Jackie Cooper, Jean Harlow, and the Marx Brothers.

Although the studio helped arrange for her to begin recording with a big company, Judy was disappointed to find at first that she wasn't asked to appear in any movies. She was kept busy, however. Every morning she went to the little red M-G-M schoolhouse with Mickey Rooney, Deanna Durbin, and the studio's other child actors. There she studied the same subjects she would have pursued in an ordinary school. In the afternoons she was given lessons in singing, dancing, acting, and diction, and she was also taught how to walk, put on makeup, and conduct herself during interviews.

Judy had been at the studio for less than two months when her father suddenly became very ill and then died. Judy was inconsolable for a long time about her father's death and for the rest of her life she was often to say, "My father's death was the most terrible thing that ever happened to me." Although she returned to work soon after the funeral, Judy no longer was a happy child. She also began to have trouble sleeping.

In the summer of 1936, when Judy turned fourteen, she and Deanna Durbin made a short musical film called *Every Sunday*. People in the movie business began to take note of her, and later that year she was loaned to Twentieth Century–Fox to act and sing several songs in her first full-length film, a football comedy with Betty Grable called *Pigskin Parade*. Judy's home studio now realized that she was a potential star. During the next two years she made five films at M-G-M, including *Love Finds Andy Hardy* in 1938 with Mickey Rooney, who had become one of her best friends.

Although Judy Garland was becoming increasingly popular, she wasn't yet a top star. Then one day in the spring of 1938, Judy was outside the studio schoolhouse playing softball with some other teenagers when a passerby suddenly stopped in his tracks. Pointing to Judy, he said, "You're Dorothy!"

"No, I'm Judy!" said the puzzled girl.

After identifying himself as a producer, the man explained that Judy was perfect to play Dorothy in an upcoming film of *The Wizard of Oz*. M-G-M had unsuccessfully tried to borrow Shirley

Temple from another studio to play Dorothy, but now Judy was considered for the role. Although at first some people thought that at sixteen she was too old to play Dorothy, Judy was so good in her screen test that she was given the part.

The Wizard of Oz was a big-budget, important film, and there were intense pressures on Judy before and during its production. One problem she had was a tendency to be a bit overweight. She was placed on a diet in which chicken soup was the only food she was allowed to eat during the day at the studio. In addition, Judy was given diet pills to help her weight-loss program along.

Studio officials were also worried that Judy's sleeping problem would cause her to look tired on camera or even get sick. Once, when Judy had a cold and couldn't appear on the set of *The Wizard of Oz* for three days, it cost the studio an extra $150,000. To make sure that she got enough sleep, the studio provided Judy with sleeping pills and sometimes put her to sleep right in the studio hospital after a long day of shooting. Then in the morning she would be given "uppers" to give her enough energy to work for the day.

While making *The Wizard of Oz,* Judy became very friendly with Margaret Hamilton, a former kindergarten teacher, who was portraying the Wicked Witch of the West. When Margaret Hamilton asked Judy why she was taking so many pills, the sixteen-year-old girl answered, "I don't seem to be able to go to sleep or wake up without them."

When *The Wizard of Oz* was released in August 1939, Judy Garland became very famous. She won a special Academy Award for her performance and was hailed for both her singing and her acting. The song "Over the Rainbow," which Judy sang in the movie, was also a big hit record and helped make her a popular recording star.

Unfortunately, Judy Garland had a very unhappy adult life. She had become addicted to various kinds of pills as a teenager, and she never overcame her addiction. She died, shortly after her forty-seventh birthday, of a drug overdose, leaving behind a long list of hit movies and records. Among her films were *Babes in Arms, Ziegfeld Girl, Life Begins for Andy Hardy, For Me and My Gal, Meet Me in St. Louis, Easter Parade, A Star is Born,* and *A Child is Waiting.*

Shirley Temple

(born in 1928)

As she and her mother waited in the lobby of the Beverly Hills movie theater for the next show to begin, five-year-old Shirley Temple looked at the wall posters that advertised coming attractions. Shirley was so excited at seeing the drawings and photographs of the movie stars that she hummed to herself and did a few dance steps while moving from poster to poster.

The little girl was studying a poster when a man asked, "How did you learn to dance so well?"

"I go to dancing school."

"Who brought you here?" the man continued.

"My mother," answered the little girl, pointing to the tall woman standing nearby.

After the man introduced himself to Mrs. Temple, the two adults went off a little way to talk. The man, who was a songwriter for a major motion picture studio, said that he thought Shirley was perfect for a role in an upcoming movie. Mrs. Temple and the man then made an appointment for Shirley to be tested for the part at the studio.

Born and raised not far from Hollywood in Santa Monica, California, Shirley Temple had been told how beautiful she was and how marvelously she sang and danced for as long as she could remember. At the age of three, she had been spotted by a movie director at her dancing school, and this had led to her appearance in several minor films. However, the audition promised by the songwriter was Shirley's first chance to land a good role in a big picture.

Several days after the encounter in the theater, Shirley and her mother arrived at the studio for the test. Shirley made a tremendous impression on the studio executives as she sang and danced on the top of a large piano. Later Mrs. Temple told Shirley that the famous actor Harold Lloyd had said, "My God, another Coogan!" while watching her. Lloyd had been referring to Jackie Coogan, one of the most popular child movie stars of the time.

Shirley was given a contract to appear in *Stand Up and Cheer,* a musical film starring Warner Baxter and James Dunn. Shirley was able to miss school during the making of the movie, and there were several other pluses about the job. For one thing, she met Will Rogers, the famous humorist, who had helped write the script. For another, Shirley was paid $150 a week — an astronomical salary during those days of the Great Depression.

Every day while *Stand Up and Cheer* was being shot, Shirley's mother brought her to the studio and helped her practice the song she was to sing near the end of the movie. Finally the day came when the director called, "Shirley, we're ready for you!" With her mother just out of camera range, Shirley tap-danced onto the stage and then sang a song called "Baby, Take a Bow."

When the studio executives viewed the "rushes" of Shirley's scene, they knew they had a new star. Shirley's dimples, curls, and smile were even more adorable on the screen than they were in real life. Not only that; her dancing was outstanding, her voice was distinctive and easily understood, and she moved with the sureness of a veteran actress.

The studio executives were soon proven right about Shirley. Across the United States and everywhere else where American movies were shown, people who saw *Stand Up and Cheer* immediately fell in love with the dimpled little girl.

After *Stand Up and Cheer*, Shirley Temple made six more features in 1934, including *Little Miss Marker* and *Bright Eyes*. During this, her first year as a star, the formula for Shirley Temple movies was established. Shirley usually played a cute, intelligent, spunky, and outspoken little girl who was alone in the world except for her father, guardian, or crusty old grandfather. Generally the adults in the pictures had big problems — with finances, the law, or hostile natives — that Shirley helped solve while dancing and singing at strategic points in the action.

As Shirley became more and more popular, her real life began to resemble a movie. Flocks of reporters came regularly to the studio to interview her, mountains of fan letters arrived each day for her, and a continual stream of sightseers parked near her house, hoping to catch just a glimpse of the famous little girl.

Not only was Shirley the most popular six-year-old in the country, she was also one of the hardest-working. Because the studio workday began early in the morning, Shirley and her mother had to awaken at dawn. While Mrs. Temple fixed Shirley's hair, the two of them practiced the little girl's lines for the day. Since Shirley didn't have time to go to school, a teacher had to be brought to the studio for her. Between her scenes, Shirley had lessons in reading, arithmetic, spelling, and all the other subjects that children in the Los Angeles public schools studied.

As Shirley's popularity continued to soar, her parents tried to maintain a normal life for her. Although she was now earning thousands of dollars per week, Mr. and Mrs. Temple put the money away for her and allowed her only five dollars for her weekly allowance. She was also given tasks at home, just as her two older brothers, Jack and George, were. Shirley's main job when she was six years old was clearing the table after dinner.

In 1935, when seven-year-old Shirley made *The Little Colonel, Our Little Girl, Curly Top,* and *The Littlest Rebel,* she was *the* most popular movie star in the world — an achievement she repeated for the next three years. In 1935 Shirley also received the first Academy Award ever won by a child. The "Oscar" came with a citation that read: "The award is bestowed because Shirley Temple brought more happiness to millions of children and millions of grown-ups than any other child of her years in the history of the world." When the Congress of the United States called her "the most beloved individual in the world," it was probably an accurate assessment. In fact, between 1935 and 1938 Shirley Temple probably received more attention from more people than any other child ever has.

Each month during those years her studio received more than ten thousand requests for autographed pictures of Shirley. Shirley Temple fan clubs — with total membership eventually reaching four million — sprang up in dozens of countries. When Shirley celebrated her ninth birthday, she was sent more than 135,000 presents, including hundreds of dolls and even a live baby kangaroo. Numerous products were named after her, including dolls, toys, dresses, and drinking mugs.

How had the little girl achieved such incredible popularity? Film critics, sociologists, and Shirley's fellow actors tried to analyze the reasons. Frank Morgan, who acted with her in *Dimples* and later played the wizard in *The Wizard of Oz,* thought the secret was her acting ability. The critic Bosley Crowther, who called Shirley a "miracle child," thought that her lovable on-screen personality was the key. Sociologists pointed out that the Depression conditions of the 1930s helped make Shirley so popular. The millions of people who were having trouble paying their rent in those years enjoyed watching a little girl who conquered her problems so cheerfully and bravely.

Between her salary from her movies and the money earned from promoting products, Shirley Temple became very rich. In 1937, when she was just nine years old, Shirley earned $307,014, making her the seventh highest paid individual in the

United States. Thanks to the fortune that she had earned, the Temples were able to move into a mansion in Los Angeles. On the grounds, Shirley had her own "playhouse," which was so big and so well equipped that, many years later when she got married, she and her husband lived in it for a while.

Despite this storybook life, fame had several drawbacks. Because of the possibility that she would be kidnapped for ransom, Shirley couldn't go out to play with other children without supervision. Although most of her fans politely asked for autographs, a few yanked at her hair and clothes in pursuit of a genuine Shirley Temple curl or scrap of clothing. Even her father had trouble because of Shirley's fame. The problem was that parents would bring their children into the bank where Mr. Temple worked and have them sing and dance in the hope that he could get them jobs in Hollywood. Finally, Mr. Temple left his bank job to manage Shirley's finances.

When reporters asked Shirley what she thought about being mobbed everywhere she went, she answered, "I don't mind at all. It's part of the job." But there were times when Shirley showed that she was really a regular little kid and not the perpetually bright and cheerful little girl people saw on-screen. Occasionally she couldn't help yelling "Hurry up!" to the tenth photographer or reporter who had come to visit her on a particular day. She also liked to tease her directors by going around the set and imitating the way they walked and spoke.

The one time Shirley did something really naughty was at a barbecue at the home of President Franklin D. Roosevelt and his wife, Eleanor Roosevelt, in New York State. As the adult guests talked, Shirley observed Mrs. Roosevelt bending over the lamb chops that she was broiling. Something about the sight of the First Lady's large rear end prompted Shirley to pick a pebble off the ground, place it in her slingshot, and send it flying. By the time the pebble struck the First Lady's backside, Shirley had put her slingshot away and had an angelic look on her face.

The Secret Service men who guarded the President's family couldn't figure out where the pebble had come from, and neither could Mrs. Roosevelt, but Mrs. Temple knew. When the Temples returned to their hotel, her mother asked Shirley why she had done it. "I just couldn't resist!" Shirley explained, before receiving her spanking.

As the 1930s drew to a close, Shirley's popularity declined. People didn't find the eleven-year-old Shirley nearly as cute and appealing as the six-year-old Shirley. Although she sporadically made movies until the age of twenty-one and hosted several TV shows after that, Shirley Temple's career as a major star was over by the time she was thirteen.

Shirley Temple did not have the difficulty facing real life that so many movie stars — especially child stars — have experienced after leaving the limelight. She developed a strong interest in politics, and in 1967 she ran, unsuccessfully, for a seat in the United States House of Representatives. Later, the most popular child star of all time served as a United States delegate to the General Assembly of the United Nations, and also as ambassador to the African country of Ghana.

Anne Frank

(1929–1945)

On June 12, 1942, Anne Frank's parents gave her a diary for her thirteenth birthday. In her first entries Anne described the boys she liked, insisted that teachers were "the greatest freaks on earth," and confessed that her math teacher had dubbed her the "Incurable Chatterbox." Anne also boasted about doing well on her final exams at school and made it clear that she expected to have an enjoyable summer.

Anne's hopes for the summer were crushed one day in early July when she was out on a walk with her father. Suddenly Mr. Frank told her that the family would soon have to go into hiding. When

Anne asked why, he explained that it was to avoid being captured by the Germans.

"But, Daddy, when would it be?" Anne asked.

"Don't you worry about it, we shall arrange everything," he replied.

Anne Frank was just one among many millions of people whose lives were being destroyed by World War II (1939–1945), a conflict that eventually involved fifty-nine countries. On one side of this struggle were the "Allies," which included France, Great Britain, the Soviet Union, the United States, and also the Netherlands, the small country where Anne lived. On the other side were Germany, Italy, Japan, and the other "Axis" nations.

World War II was one of the most horrifying wars in human history. More than sixteen million soldiers, and about that many civilians, eventually died in the conflict. The biggest loss of civilian lives occurred among the European Jewish people. About six million European Jews — roughly 60 percent of all the Jews living on the continent — were killed by the German Nazis.

The Nazi leader, Adolf Hitler, had convinced most of the German people that the Jews were responsible for Germany's troubles. Before the start of World War II, the Nazis had seized the property of German Jews and had banned them from public schools. To escape this persecution, thousands of Jews had left Germany during the 1930s. In 1933, when Anne had been four and her sister Margot seven, the Franks had moved from Frankfurt, Germany, to Amsterdam in the Netherlands. Margot and Anne had been welcomed warmly by their Dutch schoolmates and neighbors. By that July day of 1942 when their father said they would "soon have to go into hiding," the two girls could barely remember having lived anywhere but in the Netherlands.

The reason the Franks had to go into hiding was that by 1942 the Nazis were systematically working to exterminate all the Jewish people. In Germany and in countries conquered by Germany, the Nazis arrested every Jewish man, woman, and child they could find. The Nazis sent them to prisons known as concentration camps. The weaker people were often killed right away at the concentration camps, while the stronger ones were forced to work for the Nazis for a while, but the result was almost always the same. Those men, women, and children who didn't die of hunger, cold, or disease were herded into chambers where they were killed with poison gas. At just one concentration camp, the infamous Auschwitz in Poland, more than two and a half million persons, most of them Jews, were murdered within several years. Although the Jews were their main civilian target, the Nazis also murdered millions of others, including Gypsies, Polish people, Czechoslovakians, Russians, and people who tried to help the Jews.

The Nazis had conquered the Netherlands in May 1940, and by the summer of 1942 they had begun to round up that country's Jewish people and send them to the death camps. Realizing what was happening, Mr. Frank had decided that his family would hide in an unused portion of his business building with another Jewish family, the Van Daans. Mr. Frank and Mr. Van Daan, who were business partners, informed several people at their office of these plans. At the risk of their own lives these people swore to keep the secret and to bring the four Franks and the three Van Daans food for the duration of the war.

In her diary Anne described how she, Margot, and their parents packed their belongings into satchels and shopping bags and left their home at dawn on July 6, 1942. Probably quite a few Dutch people who saw the Franks walking down the street with their belongings on that Monday morning realized that they were going into hiding. But no one told the Nazis about the man, woman, and two girls who entered the office at 263 Prinsengracht and didn't come out.

Anne, Margot, and their parents climbed to the second floor and opened the gray door that led to their hiding place. As Anne unpacked, she felt much better than she'd expected about the situation. Chairs, sofas, and cots had been moved from the offices into the hiding place. There was a bathroom up there, and also — in a room that had been used as a laboratory — a sink and stove. The Franks fixed up their new home as nicely as they could, and then a large cupboard was placed outside the entrance to hide it.

Each day two men and two women helpers in the office sneaked upstairs to bring the Franks food, books, and newspapers. Aside from those visits, Anne and her family were totally cut off from other people. All day they had to remain quiet so that the office workers below wouldn't hear them. If they wanted to flush the toilet, they had to wait until the evening when everyone had left the office. After several days, Anne described the oppressiveness of her life in hiding:

> We have forbidden Margot to cough at night, although she has a bad cold, and make her swallow large doses of codeine. I am looking for Tuesday when the Van Daans arrive; it will be much more fun and not so quiet. It is the silence that frightens me so in the evenings and at night. . . . I can't tell you how oppressive it is *never* to be able to go outdoors, also I'm very afraid that we shall be discovered and be shot. That is not exactly a pleasant prospect. We have to whisper and tread lightly during the day, otherwise the people in the warehouse might hear us.

Despite these conditions, Mr. and Mrs. Frank tried to make life as normal as possible in the "Secret Annexe," as Anne called their hiding place. Every day Mr. Frank gave Anne and Margot lessons in such subjects as English, French, algebra, geography, and history. When the girls finished their schoolwork they passed the time by reading and playing Monopoly. Anne also spent a great deal of time composing stories and writing in her diary.

On the Franks' eighth day of hiding the Van Daans arrived and moved into the empty third-floor rooms. Anne had looked forward to meeting the Van Daans' fifteen-year-old son, Peter, but at first he disappointed her. Anne thought he was immature and described him as a "rather soft, shy, gawky youth; can't expect much from his company."

When Anne Frank and her family had been in hiding for four months they arranged through their helpers to take in another person, a fifty-four-year-old dentist named Albert Dussel. Anne wrote in her diary that she wasn't very happy about sharing her room with the middle-aged dentist, but "If we can save someone, then everything else is of secondary importance."

About the time of Dr. Dussel's arrival, the Nazis began making large-scale arrests of Jewish people in the Netherlands. On some nights the eight people in the "Secret Annexe" looked out the window and watched as their Jewish friends and neighbors were driven out onto the streets. On November 19, 1942, Anne described these gruesome roundups:

> The Germans ring at every front door to inquire if there are any Jews living in the house. If there are, then the whole family has to go at once. If they don't find any, they go on to the next house. No one has a chance of evading them unless one goes into hiding. . . . In the evenings when it's dark, I often see rows of good, innocent people accompanied by crying children, walking on and on . . . bullied and knocked about until they almost drop. No one is spared — old people, babies, expectant mothers, the sick — each and all join in the march of death. . . .
>
> I feel wicked sleeping in a warm bed, while my dearest friends have been knocked down or have fallen into a gutter somewhere out in the cold night. I get frightened when I think of close friends who have now been delivered into the hands of the cruelest brutes that walk the earth. And all because they are Jews!

Despite her worries about the Nazis, Anne was still a typical teenager in many ways. Her diary entries show that she was constantly evaluating the relationships within her family, and that she was usually upset about her conclusions. For one thing, she thought that her parents — especially her mother — preferred Margot to her. Margot had always earned top grades and was well liked by adults. Anne, whom her father called "a real problem child," was very sarcastic and often wrote stories or daydreamed when she was supposed to be studying.

When Anne daydreamed, it was often about boys. Although she had had "strings of boy friends" in the outside world, Anne could only fantasize about boys in the "Secret Annexe" — until the day she discovered that Peter Van Daan was pretty interesting after all.

In early 1944, when the Franks and the Van Daans had been in hiding for a year and a half, Anne realized that Peter was staring at her during meals. She was surprised, because she had thought that Peter had a crush on Margot. When Anne and Peter began to discuss their studies, Anne found that she very much enjoyed the young man's company. Soon the two of them were getting together in out-of-the-way parts of the "Secret Annexe" to talk about what they wanted to do when they returned to the outside world and to exchange a few kisses. Anne wasn't sure what being in love meant, and at times she insisted that she wasn't in love with Peter, but at other times she was sure that she was!

Anne also liked to daydream about what she

would do if she got the chance to grow up. By April of 1944, when she was not quite fifteen years old, Anne had chosen her future career:

> I must work . . . to become a journalist, because that's what I want! I know that I can write, a couple of my stories are good, my descriptions of the "Secret Annexe" are humorous, there's a lot in my diary that speaks, but — whether I have real talent remains to be seen. . . .
>
> I want to go on living even after my death! And therefore I am grateful to God for giving me this gift, this possibility of developing myself and of writing, of expressing all that is in me.
>
> I can shake off everything if I write; my sorrows disappear, my courage is reborn. But, and that is the great question, will I ever be able to write anything great, will I ever become a journalist or a writer? I hope so, oh, I hope so very much, for I can recapture everything when I write, my thoughts, my ideals and my fantasies.

Anne often lay in bed at night thinking about the future of something more important than herself: the entire human race. As warplanes droned over the rooftops of Amsterdam, Anne worried that humanity was intent on destroying itself, a fear that she expressed in her diary on May 3, 1944:

> As you can easily imagine we often ask ourselves here despairingly: "What, oh, what is the use of the war? Why can't people live peacefully together? Why all this destruction?"
>
> The question is very understandable, but no one has found a satisfactory answer to it so far. Yes, why do they make still more gigantic planes, still heavier bombs . . . ? Why should millions be spent daily on the war and yet there's not a penny available for medical services, artists, or for poor people?
>
> Why do some people have to starve, while there are surpluses rotting in other parts of the world? Oh, why are people so crazy?

By the summer of 1944 it appeared that Germany and the other Axis countries would soon lose the war, and so the eight people in the "Secret Annexe" began to talk of the time when they would return to the outside world. On July 15, 1944, Anne displayed her optimism about the future when she wrote:

> It's really a wonder that I haven't dropped all my ideals, because they seem so absurd and impossible to carry out. Yet I keep them, be-

cause in spite of everything I still believe that
people are really good at heart. I simply can't
build up my hopes on a foundation consisting
of confusion, misery, and death. I see the world
gradually being turned into a wilderness, I
hear the ever approaching thunder, which will
destroy us too, I can feel the sufferings of
millions and yet, if I look up into the heavens,
I think that it will all come right, that this
cruelty too will end, and that peace and tran-
quillity will return again.

Twenty days after Anne wrote those words,
the door to the "Secret Annexe" was suddenly thrown
open and five men carrying pistols burst inside. For
a second the eight Jewish people stared in surprise
at the intruders, and then they realized that the
Gestapo (Nazi secret police) had arrived. Someone — it was never learned who — had told the Nazis
of their whereabouts.

Anne stood there watching as the Nazis ripped
people's jewelry right off their necks and hands and
gathered up their other valuables. She saw one of
the Nazis pick up her father's briefcase containing
her diary and stories and dump the papers onto
the floor. The men shoved the valuables they had
grabbed into the briefcase and then herded the
eight people downstairs into a waiting van.

Anne Frank and the seven others were taken

to Gestapo headquarters and from there they were sent to concentration camps. All but Anne's father were soon dead. Mrs. Frank and Mr. Van Daan died at Auschwitz. Mrs. Van Daan, Margot Frank, and Anne Frank died at the concentration camp called Belsen in Germany. Dr. Dussel died at the Neuengamme concentration camp in Germany. When the Nazis abandoned Auschwitz in early 1945 to escape the advancing Allied soldiers, they took Peter Van Daan with them, probably to carry supplies. He was never heard from again. The sole survivor among the eight people from the "Secret Annexe" was Mr. Frank, who was freed by the Russian soldiers who arrived at Auschwitz in January 1945.

Although Anne Frank was dead, her thoughts were preserved in the form of those papers the Nazis had dumped onto the floor of the "Secret Annexe." The two men who had helped the people in the "Secret Annexe" were jailed, but the two women helpers, Miep van Santen and Elli Vossen, avoided arrest. Not long after Anne and the others had been taken away, Miep and Elli went up into the hiding place to gather whatever of the people's possessions they could find. Scattered on the floor among the clothes and other items were Anne Frank's diary and stories, which they locked up in the office safe.

When Mr. Frank returned to Amsterdam near

the end of the war, Miep and Elli gave him his dead daughter's diary and papers. After reading Anne's diary, Mr. Frank decided that other people should read it, too, so he arranged to have it published.

Many millions of persons of all ages and countries have read *The Diary of a Young Girl,* which is considered one of the most important documents ever produced during wartime. The diary of the girl who wanted "to go on living even after my death" reminds us of the unique individuality of each person who has ever died in a war.

Muhammad Adh-Dhîb

(born in 1931 or 1932)

Worried-looking men in white robes were scrambling along the cliffs near the Dead Sea's northwestern shore. In their hands the men were carrying what looked like ordinary clay jars, but there was a treasure inside these jars. It wasn't a treasure of gold or silver. The jars contained biblical manuscripts that had been painstakingly copied over a two-hundred-year period.

The men belonged to a Jewish sect called the Essenes and lived in the small community now called Khirbat Qumran, about fifteen miles east of Jerusalem. The Essenes had separated themselves from their fellow Jews at Jerusalem for philosophical reasons. The Essenes believed that the Jewish people no longer followed all the rules that God had spelled out in the Bible. At Khirbat Qumran and at several other small communities in Judea, the Essenes lived and worshiped as they thought the Jewish people should.

The men had given up the pursuit of worldly goods and shared whatever they had owned upon their entrance into the community. For part of the day, all the men at Khirbat Qumran studied the Bible and prayed. Since the community was self-sufficient, everyone had a job to do. Most of the men worked as farmers, millers, cooks, potters, and tailors. Those among them who had beautiful handwriting had a special job: copying the Bible. This work was one of the community's main purposes. The Essenes believed that God's messages to humanity were contained in the Bible, and that those messages had to be preserved for future generations.

Their life together was coming to an end now, however, and that was why the men were scrambling about the cliffs with the clay jars on this day in the year A.D. 68. More than a hundred years earlier, in 63 B.C., Roman soldiers had seized Judea and made it part of the Roman Empire. From time to time, small numbers of Roman soldiers had invaded Khirbat Qumran and tortured and killed the Essenes. When the men at Khirbat Qumran heard that large numbers of Roman soldiers were on their way from Jericho, just a few miles away, they knew that they had to leave. But before departing, the men placed their biblical scrolls in the jars, which they carried up to the cliffside caves. Probably to confuse anyone who wandered into the caves, they placed a number of empty jars alongside the ones containing the scrolls.

After they finished hiding their manuscripts, the men hurried down from the cliffs, gathered up their possessions, and left Khirbat Qumran forever. What became of them is not known. Perhaps they were slain by the soldiers, or perhaps they scattered to various lands, like the other Jews who were driven from Judea by the Romans.

The Essenes had chosen their hiding places well. The sun set more than half a million times without anyone's discovering the caves that held the biblical manuscripts. And when they finally were discovered, it was completely by accident.

In the spring of 1947 a fifteen-year-old goatherd named Muhammad Adh-Dhîb was tending his herd along the northwestern shore of the Dead Sea. Muhammad's people, the Taamirah tribe, were Bedouins — nomadic Arabs who moved about with their goats, sheep, and camels in search of pastureland. At about eleven o'clock on this spring morning, Muhammad counted his flock and found that one goat was missing. Ten years later, Muhammad explained what happened next in an interview that appeared in the *Journal of Near Eastern Studies:*

> I came to my companions [two other herders, who were his friends] and told them that I wanted to leave my flock with them and wanted to go out and search for the lost goat. I left them and went in search of the goat. I had to climb hills and go down into valleys. I went very far from the herdsmen. As I was roaming, I came upon a cave with its entrance open at the top like a cistern. Supposing that the goat had fallen into the cave, I started throwing in stones; and every time I threw a stone into the cave, I would hear a sound like the breaking of pottery. Then I was puzzled as to what the sound was, and I wanted to know what was in the cave . . .

Partly because Muhammad wasn't interviewed until several years later, and partly because everything he said had to be translated, exactly what happened next is not known. A London *Times* reporter who interviewed Muhammad in 1949 wrote that the young man suddenly got scared while standing at the cave entrance, ran away, and later returned with a friend named Ahmed Mohammed, who discovered the scrolls with him. However, in the interview in the *Journal of Near Eastern Studies* in 1957, Muhammad said that he made the discovery by himself:

> ... so I went down into the cave and found the pottery jars. I began to break the jars with my staff, thinking I would find treasure. However, in the first nine jars which I broke, I found little seeds of reddish color, and nothing else was in them. When I broke the tenth jar, which was the smallest of the jars, I found in it some rolled leather with scrawling on it.

Regardless of whether Muhammad found the scrolls by himself or with a friend, the important fact is that he did find them. Muhammad had attended elementary school at the Lutheran church in Bethlehem, and there he had learned about the Old and New Testaments and about the archaeological finds that were periodically made in the Holy Land. Muhammad carried the scrolls back to the tent he was sharing with his two herder friends. After examining the scrolls briefly, the three of them decided to keep them and to try to sell them in Bethlehem.

Several days later, when the boys left what the Bedouins called the "Wilderness" and returned to their people with their herds, they showed the scrolls to friends and relatives. When one of the scrolls was unwrapped, it was found to stretch all the way across the tent. Although none of Muhammad's people could identify the strange writing on the scrolls, they agreed that they might have some value to the antiquities dealers in Bethlehem. It was agreed that Muhammad, Ahmed, and the third herder would take the scrolls and try to sell them when the tribe made one of its Saturday trips into Bethlehem for farmers' market day.

One Saturday, Muhammad, Ahmed, and their friend hid the scrolls in some blankets and went with their people into Bethlehem. The reason they hid the scrolls was that, according to the law, they were supposed to turn them over to the government of Transjordan (now Jordan), the country where they had been found.

While their elders sold milk and cheese and made purchases in the marketplace, the three boys entered an antique shop. After studying the scrolls for a short while, the dealer handed them back to the boys and told them he thought they were just some fifty- or hundred-year-old Jewish Torahs with little monetary value

The boys then entered the shop of a second dealer — Khalil Iskander Shahin, who was known as Kando. Kando studied the scrolls and then asked if he could show them to Archbishop Samuel at St. Mark's Monastery in Jerusalem, to see if he wanted to purchase them for his library.

The boys agreed to leave one of the scrolls with Kando. A short time later, while the three young herdsmen were back out in the Wilderness grazing their herds, Kando brought the scroll to Jerusalem and showed it to Archbishop Samuel. The archbishop thought it was very old and said that he wanted to purchase all of the scrolls. Kando promised that he would send Muhammad and his friends to the archbishop the next time he saw them.

After Muhammad and his friends learned from Kando that Archbishop Samuel was interested in their scrolls, they went to Jerusalem and knocked on the door of St. Mark's Monastery, which is thought to stand on the site of the Last Supper. However, the monk who responded to their knocks took one look at the three rough-looking Bedouins with daggers in their belts and refused to let them inside to see Archbishop Samuel. The archbishop, who hadn't told anyone about the scrolls, had planned to meet the boys at the door himself. Through sheer bad luck, the boys had happened to come while the archbishop was at lunch!

Upon their return to the desert, Muhammad, Ahmed, and the third herdsman decided to divide up the scrolls. The third herdsman took his scrolls to an antiquities dealer who managed to sell them to Hebrew University in Jerusalem. Meanwhile, Archbishop Samuel, who felt terrible about the way the boys had been treated at his door — and worse still about not getting the scrolls — got in touch with the young herdsmen through Kando.

On August 5, 1947, Muhammad and Ahmed, accompanied by Kando, brought their scrolls for a second time to St. Mark's Monastery, and this time they were politely admitted to see Archbishop Samuel. In his book *Treasure of Qumran: My Story of the Dead Sea Scrolls,* the archbishop described the moment that he first saw the manuscripts:

> . . . I heard the story of the lost goat and the cave — this time from the boy purported to have discovered it. Then from a wrinkled, soiled bag, Kando produced not one, but *five* aged and ugly scrolls that seemed to me at the moment the most beautiful things in the world.
>
> One was quite thick and excellently preserved, with column after column of clearly defined Hebraic lettering hanging gracefully from ruled lines.

Because the archbishop believed that all the scrolls were extremely old, he offered the boys all of his own personal money. It amounted to sixty-odd dinars, worth about two hundred and fifty American dollars at the time. Muhammad and Ahmed looked at each other and then nodded. Although the money they received seemed like a lot to the boys, they could have gotten many tens of thousands of dinars for the scrolls had they known their true nature.

After several months of study, the professors at Hebrew University and the experts who came to St. Mark's Monastery concluded that the scrolls were biblical manuscripts and were far older than anyone had imagined — about two thousand years old, in fact. Archaeologists went to the region where Muhammad had found the scrolls, and in the next few years they discovered hundreds more. Because they were all found near the Dead Sea, people called them the Dead Sea Scrolls. Several of the manuscripts, including the Book of Daniel, were so old that they had been copied just a few years after the original composition! These ancient manuscripts gave scholars the opportunity to check the accuracy of modern versions of the Old Testament, which turned out to be remarkably similar.

In 1948 — the year after Muhammad Adh-Dhîb found the first Dead Sea Scrolls — the Jewish people finally regained their homeland when the country of Israel was created. The Dead Sea Scrolls, which are the oldest biblical manuscripts ever found, are now kept in a special sanctuary called "The Shrine of the Book" in Jerusalem, Israel.

Pelé

(born in 1940)

Four-year-old Edson Arantes do Nascimento lived with his parents, sister, brother, uncle, and grandmother in a small wooden house in Bauru, a city of about a hundred thousand inhabitants in southern Brazil. Edson's father, Dondinho do Nascimento, was a professional soccer player, who earned the equivalent of about five dollars per game. Dondinho also helped support the family by doing maintenance work at a health clinic.

One of little Edson's favorite pastimes was to go to the stadium and watch his father play. Soccer, known in Brazil as *futebol,* is the country's national sport, and the fans are extremely serious about it.

When the crowds cheered Dondinho for scoring a goal, Edson would smile and say, "That's my father!" But if the spectators booed Dondinho for playing poorly, Edson would clench his fists and challenge adults five times his size to fight.

Dondinho had badly hurt his knee playing soccer back when Edson had been a baby, and this hampered his play and even caused him to walk with a limp. Edson's mother, Celeste, didn't want her children to be injured like her husband and tried to keep her children away from the game. Nonetheless, Edson played soccer whenever he had the chance.

The boys in Edson's neighborhood couldn't afford a soccer ball, but that didn't stop them from playing. They stuffed a sock with rags, strings, and crumpled newspapers and used it as a ball. Their only problem might be when Edson's father discovered that one of his socks was being kicked around on the street. If he took the sock back, the boys would have to get another "ball" from a neighborhood clothesline.

The boys had no field, so they played right out on the dusty street. The goals were the two ends of the street, and the sidewalks were the sidelines. There were few cars in the poor section of Bauru, so the boys were able to play with little disturbance until the last rays of sunlight.

Although Edson was small for his age, by his

seventh birthday he was a much better player than boys three and four years older. He could kick the ball accurately and hard, he was good at hitting it with his head, and he was so fast that he could easily steal the ball from his opponents. At home, everyone called Edson "Dico." At about the age of seven his soccer-playing friends gave him a nickname, too. They called him "Pelé," perhaps because he was so good at their pickup games, which they called *peladas.* Although at first Edson despised being called Pelé and even got into fights about the nickname, after a while he learned to tolerate it.

When Pelé was ten years old, he and his friends decided that they wanted to have a real soccer team with real equipment. A magazine was holding a contest in which anyone who assembled a complete collection of soccer cards would win a soccer ball. Pelé and his friends pooled their cards, sent them to the magazine, and soon had their first soccer ball.

The boys made shorts out of flour sacks and scrounged enough money to buy soccer shirts. They named their team the September 7th Club. "September 7th" was a street in their neighborhood that had been named for Brazil's national holiday — Independence Day. The boys elected Pelé captain and began challenging other neighborhood teams to play them.

Pelé, his little brother, Zoca, and the other boys on the September 7th team were so good that they devastated most of their opponents. Soon crowds were coming to watch them as they played in various streets and fields.

When Pelé was twelve, the mayor of Bauru sponsored a soccer tournament for the city's neighborhood teams. Pelé's team beat one opponent after another and made it to the championship game, which was held on the field where Dondinho's professional team played. When Pelé ran out to his center-forward position and saw that the five-thousand-seat stadium was jammed with screaming fans, he was nervous for the first time on a soccer field. Once the game started, however, his nervousness vanished. Then he scored a goal, and a chant that he would hear thousands of times in future years rose through the stands: "Pe-lé! Pe-lé! Pe-lé!" After Pelé's team received the championship trophy from the mayor, Dondinho came down from the stands and told him, "You played a beautiful game, Dico! I couldn't have played any better myself!"

Because Dondinho knew that his wife hated soccer, he had refrained from encouraging his boys to play it. But now that he saw how serious and talented Pelé was, Dondinho decided to give him a few soccer lessons. Dondinho showed Pelé how to kick well with both feet and gave him many other important pointers. Sometimes Pelé would go with his father to the health clinic and, while helping him wash the floors, he would ask Dondinho about the teams he had played on and the famous players he had known.

About a year after the mayor's tournament, Dondinho's team, the Bauru Athletic Club, formed a minor-league team composed of youngsters. Pelé and several of his friends were among those chosen for this team, which played its home games in front of the large crowds in the Bauru Athletic Club stadium. The coach of the team, a great retired player named Valdemar de Brito, taught Pelé how to kick the ball so that it would curve, and many other things that improved his game.

At fourteen Pelé dropped out of school and went to work sewing boots in a shoe factory. In that same year a scout for a professional team in the Brazilian city of Rio de Janeiro arrived in Bauru. The scout watched Pelé play and then asked if he wanted to try out for the professional team. Dondinho said it was fine with him, but Pelé's mother wouldn't allow him to go off to live in Rio by himself.

Pelé felt bad about having to pass up this opportunity, but he soon had another chance for a tryout. Valdemar de Brito had left Bauru to scout for the Santos Football Club, which played in a city near São Paulo. When Valdemar returned to Bauru on a visit, he stopped at Pelé's house.

"Dondinho," he said, "Santos has a fine young team and the city isn't much bigger than Bauru.

I'm sure Edson would be happy there. Let him try out."

Again Pelé's father was willing to let him go, but his mother wasn't. "Dico's still a baby, Valdemar," she said. "I don't want him to leave home yet. Who will see that he eats right? Who is going to look after his clothes?"

Valdemar left, but several days later he returned and asked Pelé's parents to accompany him to a hotel in downtown Bauru. "A call is coming from the president of the Santos Football Club and I want you to speak to him," Valdemar told Celeste do Nascimento. When the call came through, the president assured Pelé's mother that the boy would be well cared for. When his parents and Valdemar returned from the hotel, Pelé saw that his mother was crying. She told her older son that although she didn't want him to suffer because of soccer, she would give her permission because she didn't want him sewing boots for the rest of his life.

Pelé's parents borrowed some money and bought the boy new clothes for his trip to Santos. His father accompanied him on the train ride. Pelé later recalled in his autobiography that he grew very emotional when the train pulled out of his hometown, and that he said to his father: "The first money I earn I'm going to send to you to buy a house for Mama!"

Once in Santos, they went to the Santos Football Club stadium. Valdemar led Pelé and Dondinho down to the dressing room and introduced them to Luis Alonso, the Santos coach. "So you're the famous Pelé, eh?" asked the coach with a smile.

"Yes, sir," said Pelé, who was embarrassed when the players laughed at his answer. Pelé had been warned that the professionals might give him the cold shoulder, but as he met the players the opposite happened. Nearly every player came up to Dondinho and promised to keep an eye on his boy. Then Dondinho gave Pelé a hug, got on a bus, and headed back to Bauru.

Pelé was led to the team boardinghouse and given a cot. He liked his roommates and the food was fine, but he had a strong case of *saudade* (the Portuguese word for homesickness). He almost hoped that the team wouldn't want him, so that he could go home and forget about becoming a professional soccer player. But several days later, when Pelé had his tryout, the coach decided that he wanted the hundred-twenty-pound, fifteen-year-old player. Since Pelé was too young to sign a contract, he and Valdemar returned to Bauru where his parents agreed on a deal offering their son five thousand cruzeiros a month, which was then equal to about two hundred and fifty American dollars. This was a much higher salary than the average adult in Brazil earned.

Coach Alonso thought that Pelé wasn't quite

ready to play with the Santos adult professional club, so for a while he played on Santos's one amateur and two juvenile teams, which were like minor-league teams. Pelé had no trouble scoring goals, but he was having trouble getting over his homesickness. Twice he packed his suitcase and started to head for home. Both times he was talked out of leaving by the clubhouse maintenance man.

One day one of the Santos professionals broke his leg during a game. While his leg healed, the team used other players to replace him. But when the player returned to the lineup and it became evident that he could no longer perform well, Coach Alonso decided to replace him with Pelé.

It was late in the summer of 1956 when the fifteen-year-old Pelé was sent in for his first adult professional game — an exhibition match against a Swedish team. Pelé played beautifully, but when the game was over Coach Alonso found him sitting sadly in the dressing room.

"What's the matter?" asked the coach.

"I didn't make any goals," answered Pelé.

The coach laughed and said, "You don't make goals every day. It would be nice, but it just doesn't happen."

A few days later, on Independence Day, September 7, 1956, Pelé scored his first professional soccer goal in a 7–1 Santos victory in a league game. Pelé almost disproved his coach's comment about not making goals "every day"; by the end of 1957 he had scored sixty-seven goals in seventy-five games.

By the time Pelé's first year as a professional was over, he had made such a big impression throughout Brazil that he was chosen to play for his country's team in the most important international soccer tournament, the World Cup. In 1958, when Pelé was just seventeen years old, he traveled with the Brazilian national team to Sweden. In one early game in the tournament, Pelé scored the only goal in his team's victory against Wales. In the championship game against Sweden, Pelé scored two goals, and Brazil won the world title by a score of 5–2.

Pelé did many more amazing things in his soccer career. He scored 1,281 goals in the 1,363 professional games of his twenty-two-year professional career, which included several seasons with the New York Cosmos in the North American Soccer League. Pelé also led Brazil to two more World Cup championships, in 1962 and 1970.

In the opinion of many people, Pelé was not only the greatest soccer player of all time, but the greatest athlete in any sport. He was so popular that kings, queens, and presidents came to soccer games just to watch him play, cease-fires in wars were arranged so that people on both sides could watch him, and dozens of songs were written in many languages about him. Despite these great accomplishments, one event that didn't make headlines gave him a special pleasure. Just as he'd promised his father on the train, Pelé took some of the first money he earned as a professional and bought a new home for his family.

Muhammad Ali

(born Cassius Clay in 1942)

Twelve-year-old Cassius Clay and his best friend, Johnny Willis, were riding around on their bicycles in their hometown of Louisville, Kentucky, when it began to rain. Cassius and Johnny didn't want to ride home in the downpour, so they pedaled over to the Columbia Auditorium, where the Louisville Home Show was being held.

The boys parked their bikes in a dry spot outside the auditorium and went inside. For the next several hours they looked at the exhibits while gorging themselves on free popcorn, hot dogs, and candy. It was already beginning to get dark when Cassius realized that it was past the time for him to be home.

Once outside, the boys found Johnny's bike where he'd left it, but Cassius's new red Schwinn with the chrome trim and spotlight was gone. Cassius and Johnny ran up and down the street asking people if they had seen anyone riding away on a new red Schwinn. No one had, but one person told them to go downstairs in the auditorium and ask for a policeman named Joe Martin.

Cassius and Johnny raced downstairs into the Columbia gym, where they found Officer Martin supervising about ten boys in his amateur boxing class. "My new Schwinn's gone!" Cassius told the off-duty policeman. "Someone stole it from right outside the building!"

While Officer Martin filled out a report, Cassius watched the boys in the gym shadowbox, hit the speed bags, and skip rope. Many years later, in his autobiography, *The Greatest,* he explained how he temporarily forgot about the bike while in the gym:

> There were about ten boxers in the gym, some hitting the speed bag, some in the ring, sparring, some jumping rope. I stood there, smelling the sweat and rubbing alcohol, and a feeling of awe came over me. One slim boy shadowboxing in the ring was throwing punches almost too fast for my eyes to follow.

Before Cassius left the gym, Officer Martin handed him a piece of paper. "We have boxing every night, Monday through Friday, from six to eight. Here's an application in case you want to join up."

Cassius stuffed the application into his pocket and rode home on the back of Johnny's bike. When Cassius got home, his father yelled at him for having left his bike in an unsafe place. Relieved at getting off without a more severe punishment, Cassius forgot about boxing for a few days.

That Saturday night the Clay family was watching television when a boxing show called "Tomorrow's Champions" came on station WAVE. Between rounds, the camera showed a close-up of a familiar face talking to one of the boxers.

"Bird!" Cassius said to his mother. "That man said he could teach me to box. Did you see a piece of paper I had in my pants pocket?"

Mrs. Clay, who was called "Bird" by Cassius and his younger brother, Rudy, because they claimed she was "as sweet and pretty as a bird," had found the application while doing the laundry. "You want to be a boxer?" asked Mrs. Clay, who didn't want Cassius to participate in the brutal sport. When Cassius told her he did, she asked, "How are you going to get there? Your bike is gone."

"I'll borrow somebody's bike," Cassius answered.

Mrs. Clay asked her husband what he thought about Cassius's boxing. Cassius wasn't a wild kid, but he did cause his share of trouble. He and Rudy sometimes got into stone-throwing fights out on the streets with the neighborhood boys. Cassius also liked to play practical jokes. One of his favorites was to run a string all the way from his parents' bedroom curtain into his own room. Then in the middle of the night he'd pull the string to make his parents' curtain jump around. Possibly thinking about such stunts, Mr. Clay said that anything that kept Cassius out of trouble was all right with him.

Several evenings later, Cassius went down to the gym. He was so eager to put on the gloves that he immediately challenged a bigger boy, who there-upon bloodied Cassius's nose. Fortunately, another boy rushed in, pulled Cassius away, and advised him to take some boxing lessons — especially if he was going to pick on an older guy.

When Mr. Martin arrived, Cassius had his first boxing lesson. From that day on, Cassius came to the gym at opening time and stayed until it closed. Mr. Martin taught Cassius the proper stance, how to punch, how to throw a series of punches called combinations, how to do a fake punch, or feint. At first Mr. Martin didn't think that Cassius had any more talent than the dozens of other young boxers who came to the gym, but he did appreciate Cassius's dedication.

"I like the way you work at it," Mr. Martin

would say, as Cassius skipped rope or hit the speed bag. "If you keep it up you might be pretty good someday."

In addition to being a policeman and a boxing coach, Mr. Martin was promoter and matchmaker for the Louisville television show "Tomorrow's Champions." One day when Cassius had been coming to the gym for about two months, Mr. Martin told him he was ready to box on TV for four dollars a bout. Cassius's mother made only a few dollars a day cleaning houses, and his father didn't earn much painting signs. Four dollars for doing something he loved sounded like a fortune to Cassius.

All week before his first bout, Cassius reminded his friends and relatives to watch the show on Saturday night. He even knocked on the doors of people he barely knew, to promote his first boxing match. "I'm Cassius Clay, and I'm boxing this Saturday night on TV," he would say, flashing his sweetest smile. Some of the people slammed the door in Cassius's face, but none of them forgot him. No doubt many of those who had heard Cassius brag turned on their TVs that November Saturday to see if he could back up his boasts.

Cassius, twelve years old and weighing not much more than a hundred pounds, fought a boy named Ronny O'Keefe in that first match. Both boys were so excited by the television lights and cameras that they forgot most of what they knew about the sport and began flailing away at each other the moment the bell rang. At the end of the three rounds, the referee and the two judges voted to determine the winner. Cassius won by a 2–1 vote — a "split decision."

After that, Cassius became a regular on "Tomorrow's Champions," and soon grew to relish the lights and the cameras. All week he would practice at the gym and brag to everyone he knew about how he was going to "whup" his foe on Saturday night. Usually he did just that, but on the rare occasions when he lost Cassius always congratulated his opponent and was a perfect gentleman about it.

One day when Cassius was thirteen, he was riding his new little motor scooter down the street when he passed a car in which a bunch of people were listening to a boxing match. Cassius stopped his scooter and listened. When the fight was over, he heard the ring announcer say: "The winner, and still heavyweight champion of the world — *Rocky Marciano!*" Cassius later remembered feeling "a cold chill shoot through my bones" upon hearing those words. At that moment he made up his mind that someday he would be the heavyweight champion of the world.

Now that he had a goal, Cassius worked harder than ever. He read about boxing, talked to every boxer he could find, and carefully observed other fighters. He even incorporated some of his opponents' best moves into his own boxing style.

As he boxed on TV and in various gyms in the Louisville area, Cassius noticed that some of the best young boxers had been trained by a coach named Fred Stoner. One night Cassius walked over to the church basement where Mr. Stoner taught boxing.

"Have you ever watched me fight on TV?" Cassius asked.

"Yes I have, and I know you've got courage," answered Mr. Stoner, who was black like Cassius. "You've got the will, but you don't have the skill. If you want to come here, I'll teach you what I know."

Boxing now began to dominate Cassius's entire day. He worked out at Mr. Martin's gym from six to eight in the evening. Then he rode his motor scooter across town to the Grace Community Center, where he trained until midnight with Mr. Stoner, who was a very strict coach.

"One hundred push-ups!" Mr. Stoner would tell his boxing students. Once they completed the push-ups the coach would say, "One hundred knee bends!" followed by "Two hundred left jabs!" and "Two hundred right crosses!" All this exercise and practice helped Cassius improve his endurance, timing, and rhythm. Mr. Stoner also taught the boys some fancy footwork. Soon Cassius found that he could stay out of reach of a tough opponent by dancing around the ring. Then at the right moment he would dance in and — POW! — put his foe away with a lightning-fast flurry of punches.

Although Cassius was a superb student of boxing, he was a poor one at school. After going to bed after midnight, he arose at five to run in a nearby park. Then instead of boarding the bus like his classmates, Cassius raced it the entire three miles to school. Upon reaching his high school, Cassius often dozed through his classes. Even when he managed to stay awake at school, Cassius daydreamed about boxing or drew pictures of himself wearing a boxing robe with the words "WORLD HEAVYWEIGHT CHAMPION" on it.

When Cassius was fourteen years old, Mr. Martin entered him in the Golden Gloves, an amateur boxing tournament held in various cities around the United States. Cassius entered the novice (beginner) division and defeated one boy after another to take the title. All his life, Cassius had been called "GG" by his parents because "GG" had been the first thing he'd said as a baby. When Cassius brought home his trophy, his parents joked that "GG" had been his way of saying "Golden Gloves" as a baby.

During the next year, 1957, fifteen-year-old Cassius began to prove that he was going to be much more than just a good boxer. He now weighed about a hundred and fifty pounds and could outthink, outtalk, outpsych, outbox, and outlast virtually all of his opponents. However, early in the year he received some news that threatened to put a sudden end to his boxing career.

Cassius was undergoing a prefight medical examination when a doctor discovered that he had developed a heart murmur, a condition that can be anything from insignificant to very serious, depending on the cause. The doctors ordered Cassius to give up boxing until the nature of the murmur could be determined. For four months Cassius had to stay away from his favorite activity and go for periodic medical checkups. Fortunately, just as he was beginning to think that he would never be allowed to box again, the murmur disappeared.

After working himself back into shape, sixteen-year-old Cassius Clay entered the Louisville Golden Gloves and won the light-heavyweight championship. Many people expected Cassius to go on to win the national light-heavyweight Golden Gloves championship in 1958, but that didn't happen. In the quarterfinals, Kent Green, the eventual winner of the title, hit Cassius hard in the midsection. When Joe Martin saw that his fighter was hurt, he signaled the referee to stop the bout.

"Next year that Golden Gloves championship is mine!" Cassius vowed after this, his first major defeat.

In March 1959 he delivered on that promise.

In front of more than eleven thousand people at the Chicago Stadium, Cassius Clay beat Jeff Davis of Nashville, Tennessee, to win the national light-heavyweight Golden Gloves crown. The following month seventeen-year-old Cassius won the Amateur Athletic Union's national light-heavyweight title.

Cassius Clay went on to enjoy great fame and fortune as a boxer. At eighteen he won the light-heavyweight gold medal at the Olympic games. He then became a professional and eventually won the heavyweight boxing championship of the world four separate times. Even people who didn't like boxing followed his career because of the graceful way he danced in the ring and the funny rhyming boasts he made up before each fight.

The first time Cassius Clay (who soon changed his name to Muhammad Ali for religious reasons) won the world heavyweight crown was on February 25, 1964, when he knocked out Sonny Liston. Standing in the center of the ring, the happy young boxer heard the announcer say the words that he had awaited for nearly half his life:

"The winner, and new heavyweight champion of the world — *CASSIUS CLAY!*"

Bobby Fischer

(born in 1943)

During vacations, after school, and on weekends, eleven-year-old Joan Fischer often baby-sat for her little brother, Bobby, while their mother went to work. To keep the six-year-old occupied, Joan played Monopoly, Parcheesi, and other games with him. One day in 1949 Joan bought an inexpensive chess set at the candy store beneath their Brooklyn, New York, apartment. After reading the directions on the box lid, Joan and Bobby started playing. Bobby was immediately intrigued by chess and was soon beating his big sister at it regularly.

Later in the year Bobby, Joan, and their mother spent a summer vacation at Patchogue on Long

Island. It happened that someone had left a book on chess in the cottage where they were staying. Bobby studied the book throughout the vacation, and when the Fischers returned home he carried it around to read wherever he went.

Searching for a place where Bobby might learn more about chess, Mrs. Fischer began taking him to the Brooklyn Chess Club when he was seven years old. There Bobby played people old enough to be his grandparents and read every book on chess he could find. The club's president, Carmine Nigro, was so impressed by the boy's seriousness that he began taking Bobby over to his house to give him lessons along with his own son, Tommy.

The more Bobby played and read about chess, the more he loved the game. In fact, at seven Bobby already knew what he wanted to be when he grew up. When his mother took him to the supermarket, Bobby would walk up to strangers and tell them: "I'm Bobby Fischer! Someday I'm going to be chess champion of the world!"

Many children have displayed great talent or even genius at chess, an ancient game that was first played in Asia. At the age of five both José Capablanca of Cuba and Samuel Reshevsky of Poland (and later the United States) were beating good adult players. Although Bobby was an outstanding player at seven and eight, there was nothing as yet to mark him as superior to dozens of other young "chess nuts." At eleven, however, Bobby improved so rapidly that he soon became what many consider the greatest child chess player of all time.

Eleven-year-old Bobby was obsessed by chess. He took his miniature chess set and his favorite chess books and magazines with him everywhere. In school, while the other children were studying mathematics and science, Bobby would sit and read about a classic game played by Paul Morphy in the 1850s or by José Capablanca in the 1920s. At mealtime, Bobby would sit at the table next to his mother and sister and read about the Ruy López opening, Petroff's Defense, or various endgame theories. Bobby had even painted a chessboard on his bedroom ceiling. He did this so that he could stare up at the board while he was in bed and play imaginary games until he drifted off to sleep.

Mrs. Fischer was proud of Bobby's talent, but she was upset that he was excluding everything except chess from his life. He no longer played baseball or stickball with the neighborhood children, and he neglected his schoolwork. For a while Mrs. Fischer tried to limit his play, in the hope that this would get him to spend more time on his schoolwork. But Bobby was extremely independent at a young age, and his mother couldn't keep him from the game he loved. When he was supposed to be doing his homework, he would go to Central Park, where he would play for hours at the outdoor tables with chess buffs. Late into the night, he would stay up reading about chess or working out some problem at the chessboard.

When Bobby was still eleven, he entered the Brooklyn Chess Club's annual tournament and, playing against adults, he tied for third through fifth places. As lovers of the game spread the word about the young chess whiz, Bobby was invited to compete against good players at YMCAs and at other chess clubs. Bobby played everyone he could, no matter how good the opponent was or how many times he was beaten. Although he loathed losing, and sometimes cried after a defeat, Bobby realized that he could learn a lot during a loss to an outstanding player.

In the summer of 1955, shortly after his twelfth birthday, Bobby joined the prestigious Manhattan Chess Club. Although it may not seem possible, during that summer Bobby played more chess than ever before! Hour after hour he sat in the club, drinking pop and playing chess. After a few games, Bobby would relax by playing such chess variations as Rapid Transit (in which the players are allowed just ten seconds per move) or Blitz (in which the players are allowed absolutely no time between moves). While playing, Bobby lost track of the time. Often his mother had to drive the rickety old family car over to the Manhattan Chess Club in the middle of the night to bring him home.

The press began to take note of Bobby in 1955. In December of that year the *New York Times* ran a story about how Bobby had played twelve young members of the Yorktown, New York, Chess Club simultaneously and had won all twelve games. Soon newspapers and magazines throughout the country were running stories about the young chess prodigy.

In July 1956 Bobby entered his first major tournament, the U.S. Junior Championship (for people under twenty), which was held at the Franklin Mercantile Chess Club in Philadelphia. Winning eight games, losing only one, and tying one, Bobby easily won the tournament (and the prize, a portable typewriter). At thirteen, Bobby had become the youngest U.S. Junior Chess Champion ever. Bobby entered more big tournaments, and, although he didn't always win, he always made a tremendous impression on chess fans.

In the summer of 1957 Bobby went to Cleveland, where he beat out two hundred adults to win the U.S. Open chess tournament, thereby becoming the youngest American player ever to earn a major adult chess title. After this stunning victory, Bobby prepared for the biggest tournament of his young life: the U.S. Chess Championship.

Despite Bobby's growing reputation, few thought that the fourteen-year-old boy could win the tournament that crowned the champion of the entire United States. The fourteen players invited to participate in this tournament were the best of the nation's ten million chess players. Among the experts Bobby would have to beat in order to win the title were the two-time former champion Samuel Reshevsky, the former champion Arnold Denker, and Arthur Bisguier, who was the defending champion.

The tournament got under way in December 1957 at the Manhattan Chess Club and was scheduled to last until January of the next year. The format was for each participant to play a game against each of the other thirteen competitors. From the beginning, the intense boy from Brooklyn was the center of attention for several reasons. Not only was he the youngest player in the tournament, he was the only one who wore corduroy pants and a T-shirt as opposed to the standard suit and tie. Bobby soon captured people's attention for another reason — his brilliant play.

Bobby won his first game and then played to two straight draws (ties), including one against the forty-six-year-old Reshevsky, considered by many to be the best American player of the time. At that point the years of studying chess books, playing strangers in Central Park, and staring up at his ceiling chessboard far into the night began to pay off for Bobby. Biting his fingernails before each move and wandering around the smoke-filled room to study other games when it wasn't his turn, Bobby won games four and five, played to a draw in game six, and then reeled off five consecutive victories followed by another draw. Going into his thirteenth and final game, Bobby just needed a draw to assure himself of at least a tie for the championship with Samuel Reshevsky, who was in second place.

Bobby started his final game, played against Abe Turner, by moving his knight in front of his queen's bishop. Three hours later, after each player had captured a pawn, a knight, and a bishop, the players agreed to a draw. Now the only way that Reshevsky could even tie Bobby for the championship was by winning his own last game.

Too nervous to watch Reshevsky, Bobby went into a corner of the club and began playing Blitz with some friends to pass the time. After a few games of Blitz, Bobby succumbed to the suspense and walked over to check the progress of Reshevsky's game. "Reshevsky's busted," Bobby said when he returned to his friends at the Blitz table. "Lombardy's got his rooks doubled on the knight file. I give Reshevsky just ten more moves before he has to resign." A few minutes later Reshevsky gave up, and a loud cheer went up for the new chess champion of the United States: Bobby Fischer.

In a rare display of emotion, Bobby began to jump up and down and act like the extremely happy fourteen-year-old he was. But a few seconds later he calmed down, and his quiet, reserved personality returned. When a reporter asked the high-school sophomore how it felt to be the youngest player ever to become U.S. Chess Champion, Bobby said only, "It's pretty nice." When another asked how he had become so good at chess, he answered, "Practice. Study. Talent."

During the next few weeks Bobby received the kind of praise usually reserved for such sports heroes of the time as Mickey Mantle and Willie Mays. An official of the Manhattan Chess Club said, "Never before in all chess history has there been such a phenomenon." Newspapers, magazines, and TV shows referred to Bobby as a "chess prodigy," a "boy chess genius," and even the "Mozart of chess."

Bobby had more great moments in 1958. Soon after winning the U.S. championship he appeared on the TV show "I've Got a Secret" (his secret being that he was U.S. Chess Champion). He used the prize money from the show to make a June trip to Moscow, where he played against several top Russians. From there he went to a tournament in Portorož, Yugoslavia, where he tied for fifth and sixth places against some of the world's greatest players. His performance in that tournament earned Bobby the rank of International Grand Master. At fifteen, he was the youngest player in chess history ever to attain that status.

By the time Bobby was seventeen, his mother had remarried, his sister had also married, and both had moved out of the apartment. Bobby, who had quit high school, remained in the Brooklyn apartment by himself. Living on money his mother sent him, he managed to get by on his own despite his tendency to let dishes, clothes, and newspapers pile up while he played chess day and night with his friends.

By this time Bobby Fischer had a loftier ambition than the chess championship of the United States. His goal was to win the chess championship of the entire world. Although many experts expected him to attain that goal before the age of twenty, international chess rules made it difficult for a non-Russian to wrest the title from the string of Russian champions who dominated the game from the late 1930s to the 1970s.

Year after year, Bobby continued to play in tournaments — which he often won — without getting a crack at the world title. Because the prize money was usually small, Bobby supported himself by writing books and articles on chess as he traveled about to the various tournaments. Finally, in 1972, when Bobby Fischer was twenty-nine years old, he got the chance to play the world chess champion,

Boris Spassky of the Soviet Union. In a twenty-one-game battle that was the most publicized chess match of all time, Bobby Fischer became the first American chess champion of the world by defeating Spassky 12½ points to 8½ points. Bobby Fischer, who had told people more than twenty years earlier that someday he would be the world chess champion, held the world title until 1975.

Mark Whitaker

(born in 1951)

Many people remember October 4, 1957, because on that day the space age began when the Soviet Union launched Sputnik I, the first man-made satellite to orbit the earth. One person who vividly recalls that event is Mark Whitaker, who was then a six-year-old living in Bishop, Texas. In the same year, 1957, Mark saw his first comet, an event he described many years later in a letter to the author of this book:

> I was only six years old, and to this day I don't know what comet it was. I remember that just

after dark, we could go out in our front yard
and look down the street towards the western
horizon and we could see a magnificent comet
with a curved tail glowing in the twilight. Over
what seemed like a period of weeks the comet
would faithfully be there each night, its position slightly changed. It appeared to me as
if it were a celestial pinwheel, slowly cart-
wheeling through the sky providing our whole
neighborhood with a cosmic fireworks display. After this experience with a bright comet,
I wondered about how many other such spec-
tacles I had missed because of my lack of
awareness that such objects even existed.

Like many other young people of the late 1950s
and the 1960s, Mark became enthralled by all aspects of space flight and astronomy. Not only did
Mark follow every Soviet and American launch with
great interest, he and his friends used homemade
gunpowder to launch their own rockets. In addition
to reading every astronomy book owned by his school
library, Mark also read all he could find about UFOs
(unidentified flying objects) and attended every new
science-fiction movie about invaders from space that
was shown at his town's little movie theater. Sometimes at night he and his friends would lie out under
the stars and talk about the possibility of extrater-
restrial life while watching for satellites, meteors,
and — of course — UFOs.

When Mark was thirteen years old, his parents gave him a three-inch-diameter reflecting telescope for Christmas. Mark quickly learned to find the moon, planets, and several of the more prominent galaxies and nebulas with his telescope. Like most young amateur astronomers, Mark wanted to move on to a larger instrument, so that he could view his favorite celestial objects in greater detail. The aspiring astronomer soon ordered parts for a four-inch reflecting telescope, which he assembled himself.

By 1967 Mark was focusing his attention on comets — objects made of ice, gases, and dust that develop long, glowing tails when they near the sun. Because nearly all professional astronomers spend their time on much more distant objects, comet hunting has always been a good field for amateur astronomers. After reading about a young Japanese man named Kaoru Ikeya, who had discovered a comet when he was just nineteen years old, Mark began to think about discovering a comet, too. He was especially excited about the fact that comets are named for their discoverers.

To make such a discovery, a comet hunter usually must be prepared to scan the sky with a telescope night after night for several years. Luck is needed, too. Many an amateur astronomer has spotted a new comet, only to learn that one of the thousands of other comet hunters around the world was credited with the discovery several days earlier.

In late 1967 and the first half of 1968, Mark hunted for comets a few times with his telescope. His goal was to spot a little blob of light that could be seen to move over a period of hours as it slowly orbited the sun. Mark knew that such a blob would be a comet — with luck, one that had never been seen before. However, he was hampered by his own lack of a searching system. "I spent a few nights sweeping the sky with no real plan," Mark remembers about that period. "I just enjoyed the solitude, alone under the stars."

In June 1968, when Mark finished his junior year of high school, he decided to dedicate his summer to a systematic comet hunt. He also decided to follow the advice given in *New Handbook of the Heavens* and concentrate his efforts on the celestial ecliptic — the region where most objects in the solar system are located. Because comets become visible when they near the sun, he planned to observe the morning sky before sunrise and the evening sky after sunset.

On his first few comet-hunting sessions during that summer of 1968, Mark came up empty. On his third night — June 14, 1968 — Mark's hopes were raised for a few seconds when he spotted a blob of light in the constellation Serpens (the Serpent). When he looked on his star chart (a necessary aid to a comet hunter, because through a small telescope many clusters, nebulas, and galaxies look similar to comets), Mark saw that the object was just M5, a globular star cluster. Putting aside his chart, Mark returned to his telescope. In his own words, this is what happened next on that Friday night:

> I continued sweeping . . . in a north-south direction. At the end of each sweep, I would advance the telescope roughly one field diameter to the east and continue a north-south sweep. In this way, I could cover a strip of sky across the ecliptic, always moving away from the western horizon. It was the next sweep after encountering M5 that I spied a faint luminous stain on the background sky. The stain was so faint that I could not see it with direct vision. I could only see it with averted vision and even then, I wasn't sure that it was real. I knew that the object would not be identified on my crude star charts. The only way that I might ascertain whether the object was a comet or not was to look for motion. At this point I was not very excited. I knew that the odds of it being a faint galaxy or other object was much more likely than a comet.

So that he would be able to find it again, Mark memorized the position of the "luminous stain" in the sky. Fortunately, the object was just a few degrees from M5, which would serve as a guidepost for him. Mark also drew maps of the fuzzy object and the background stars as they appeared in his telescope's eyepiece. Doing this was critical. If the object was a comet, it would visibly move among the stars after a few hours as it continued on its voyage around the sun. While making his drawings, Mark began to feel excited, because it seemed to him that the object had already moved since he'd first spied it about an hour earlier.

All the next day, Mark pored over his star charts and drawings so that he would be able to find the object as soon as it was dark. Mark describes what happened on that Saturday night when he went out to the front yard with his telescope:

> I was ready and waiting as the sun set. There was some trepidation. Would I be able to find the same star field? Would the object really be there? Will it have moved? As I turned the telescope to the constellation of Serpens, I aligned on the nearest bright star to the globular cluster M5. I star hopped from this star to the cluster and then from the cluster to the star field of the previous night. The stars were there as I verified them against the drawing I had made the night before. But the object was not there! Had I imagined it? My pulse was very quick as I slowly moved the telescope to the north.
>
> Approximately three telescope fields to

the north (over 1 degree of sky) I found the faint object. I was amazed at the amount of apparent motion, but I had found a comet.

Mark excitedly ran into the house and brought his mother and father out to the front yard. After his parents had watched the comet for a while, Mark realized that he had to report it as soon as possible. He hadn't read about a comet in this particular part of the sky, but there was still a chance that it was a previously discovered comet making a return trip. It was also possible that someone else had discovered the comet just a few hours or days earlier and that Mark hadn't yet heard about it.

One of Mark's astronomy books said that the Harvard College Observatory was the official headquarters for reporting comet discoveries. It was late Saturday night by now, so Mark and his parents figured that it was a bad time to call. The next morning, with his parents' help, Mark phoned Harvard, only to learn that the Smithsonian Astrophysical Observatory was now taking comet reports. Unfortunately, the Smithsonian Observatory official in charge of comet reports was not there on that Sunday morning. Mark left a message describing the comet, and then waited for a return call.

Mark didn't know it, but approximately nine hundred miles to the northwest, in Flagstaff, Arizona, a professional astronomer named Norman G.

Thomas was studying some photographic plates of the asteroid Icarus, which was then making a close approach to the earth. Icarus happened to be in the same part of the sky as Mark's comet. Shortly after Mark phoned in his discovery, Professor Thomas noticed a streak of light on one of his plates. Suspecting that it was a comet, Professor Thomas reported his find to the Smithsonian Astrophysical Observatory, as Mark had.

On Monday or Tuesday afternoon — he can't remember which — Mark Whitaker received a long-distance phone call from the Smithsonian Observatory. He was told that the object he'd seen was a new comet and that he would receive half the credit for the discovery. Because Professor Thomas had found it on his photographic plates just a short while after Mark had first spotted the comet, it was named Comet Whitaker-Thomas. Mark Whitaker had just become the youngest person ever to discover a comet.

When the Smithsonian Observatory informed the press about Mark's discovery, the Texas teenager was besieged by reporters and photographers from newspapers and magazines. The story was run in many of the country's major newspapers, and Mark was also interviewed on television and radio. When asked about his career plans, Mark told the interviewers that he wanted to become an astronomer.

Mark maintained his interest in astronomy and even built several more telescopes, including a six-inch "rich field" instrument, which he used to search for more comets. Today Mark Whitaker lives in Louisiana with his wife and three children and works as a district manager for an oil-well service company. Although he never discovered another comet, Mark Whitaker says of his early accomplishment:

> The one memory I savor from all of this is the moment of discovery and the events of that summer. I don't really consider myself all that remarkable. Many others have discovered brighter comets or more comets. For me, the combination of a dream, the basic knowledge of astronomy gained through a hobby, and a great deal of luck came together, and gave me an experience of a lifetime.
>
> My advice to would-be discoverers is to plan carefully to maximize search time, expect a long hunt, have patience and perseverance, and to take time to enjoy the sky while hunting.

As for Mark's comet, it has an orbit that takes it much farther from the sun than the one the famous Halley's Comet travels. Comet Whitaker-Thomas won't return to our part of the solar system for millions of years — if it ever returns at all.

Nadia Comaneci

(born in 1961)

It was recess time for the schoolchildren of Oneşti, a city of forty thousand inhabitants near the Carpathian Mountains in eastern Romania, and six-year-old Nadia Comaneci was out on the playground doing a gymnastics routine with another little girl. On days when there was a soccer game at recess, Nadia was always in the center of the action — running faster, blocking more shots, and kicking more goals than anyone else. When she was in a place where there were sturdy trees for climbing, Nadia could often be seen doing acrobatics high up on a limb. Out on the playground, however, there was no soccer game on this day, and there were no good climbing trees, so Nadia was having fun doing cartwheels and ballet steps with her friend. They were in the midst of their routine when the bell rang.

As Nadia and her friend darted back toward the school with the other children, they were unaware of the tall man who was calling to them. The man followed the two little girls into the building, but in the hallway he was unable to pick them out from dozens of other children who were pouring into the rooms.

The tall man then went to the school office, where he identified himself as Bela Karolyi, an ex-athlete who was about to open a gymnastics school with his wife, Marta. Mr. Karolyi explained that he had been impressed by the gymnastics ability of the two little girls out on the playground, and then obtained permission to search for them.

The coach went into every classroom in the school, but couldn't spot the girls. He then made a second tour of the school without success. For his third attempt, Mr. Karolyi tried a new method. "Who likes gymnastics?" he asked, upon entering each room. Several years later, Bela Karolyi told magazine and newspaper writers about the moment that he located Nadia:

A third time I went in and asked, "Who likes gymnastics?" In one of the classrooms, two girls sprang up. "We! We!" they both shouted. Today, one of the girls is a very promising ballerina. The other is Nadia.

Mr. Karolyi took the girls' names and addresses and several days later he arrived at the Comanecis' house. He explained to Nadia's parents that he was scouting for promising candidates for the gymnastics school he and his wife were about to open. Mr. and Mrs. Comaneci agreed to let Nadia try out for the school.

Before being admitted to the Karolyis' school, Nadia had to pass a three-part test. She passed the fifteen-meter sprint and long-jump tests with flying colors. She was then ready for the most important test — a walk atop the balance beam four feet off the ground. Bela and Marta Karolyi felt that any girl who was afraid of walking on the narrow beam didn't have a chance of becoming a good gymnast.

Dozens of times in Oneşti and at her grandparents' house in the country, Nadia had climbed across tree limbs that were three times as high as this beam. After the little girl easily walked across the beam, Bela Karolyi congratulated her and told her she would be admitted to the new gymnastics school.

Once she entered the school, Nadia was faced with a very difficult schedule for a six-year-old. In the morning she and the twenty-five other girl gymnasts in the school were taught reading, arithmetic, and other academic subjects by the teachers on the Karolyis' staff. Then in the afternoon the girls were taught gymnastics by Bela and Marta Karolyi.

The Karolyis had some exciting new ideas about gymnastics. In the past, gymnasts had generally begun their training at about fourteen and had reached their peak in their late teens or early twenties. The Karolyis believed that gymnasts should start training at six or seven so that they would be ready for Olympic and other high-level competition at fifteen or so — the age when they thought most gymnasts achieve maximum skill. Marta Karolyi, a former gymnast, was very knowledgeable about the technical aspects of the sport. Bela, a former world champion handball player, hadn't known much about gymnastics at first, but he did know a great deal about competition and training, and as the days passed he learned from Marta about the various gymnastics events.

"If I can do it, you can!" he would tell the girls, as he worked out with them on the balance beam or the uneven parallel bars.

For the first few days the Karolyis let the girls have fun with the equipment so that they would feel comfortable with it. Soon, however, Nadia could see that Bela and Marta Karolyi were going to be the toughest teachers she had ever had. When they spoke, they demanded that the girls listen to every word, and they insisted that the girls approach gymnastics as if it were the most important thing in the world. As the girls improved, the two coaches expected them to get better and better and practice more and more.

Soon it became apparent that Nadia was the school's most promising gymnast. When Nadia was not yet eight years old, she was admitted to the new Gymnastics High School, which opened in Onești in September 1969. This school had on its staff a number of coaches, including the Karolyis. It also had teachers to provide academic lessons, doctors to maintain the athletes' health, nutritionists to provide the best diets, choreographers, and musicians to create music for the floor exercises.

Six days a week, Nadia had to awaken at six in the morning in order to get to the high school by eight. After dressing and eating breakfast, Nadia made the ten-minute walk to the school. Her first period of gymnastics practice was from eight in the morning until noon. At lunchtime, Nadia went with the other gymnasts to the cafeteria, where they ate such foods as salads, fruits, roast chicken, cheese, and milk. Whether they were in school or at home, they weren't allowed to eat fried foods or foods with artificial additives.

After lunch Nadia and the other gymnasts attended their academic classes for about four hours, and then had a rest period of several hours when they could take a nap or do their homework. After eating dinner at school, Nadia often worked out with the Karolyis for another couple of hours. Sometimes she went home to spend the night with her parents and her little brother, Adrian, but on nights when she finished practice late Nadia stayed at the school and slept in the dormitory with the out-of-town students.

Why would a seven-year-old girl subject herself to such a difficult schedule? For one thing, Nadia loved gymnastics. Patriotism was another reason for Nadia's dedication. At the time, Romania was in the process of asserting its independence from the Soviet Union, which had controlled the country from the late 1940s until about 1965. The Romanian government and people wanted to show the Soviet Union that they could compete with the giant country economically and in various other aspects of life, including athletics. The Romanians particularly wanted to do well against the Russians in the Olympic Games, which meant that promising athletes like Nadia were continually reminded that it was their patriotic duty to achieve as much as was humanly possible. There was also a more personal reason for Nadia's dedication to her sport. Athletes in her country enjoyed special treatment for themselves and their families. Nadia knew that if she became a star in gymnastics, her family would have a good chance to get a nice apartment, vacations, a fancy car, and other bonuses.

In 1970, when Nadia was eight and a half, the Karolyis decided that she and some of the other girls were ready to compete in a gymnastics meet. In June of that year they took the girls to the central Romanian city of Sibiu, where they entered them in the Romanian National Junior Gymnastics Championship.

Nadia, who was the youngest athlete at this meet, was her team's last competitor on the final piece of apparatus, the beam. All she needed was a decent score, and Onești would win the gold medal. "Get up there and show them what I've taught you," said Marta Karolyi, who was the coach for this event. "Concentrate, and don't let me down!" Mrs. Karolyi then gently pushed Nadia toward the beam.

This was the first time Nadia had performed in front of a large audience, and, perhaps from nervousness, her concentration lapsed. Suddenly, during a high leap, she fell over the left side of the beam. Red-faced with embarrassment, Nadia climbed up again and fell off the opposite side. By now some of the other competitors were hooting with laughter. For the third time she climbed up on the beam and for the third time she fell — this time with but one second remaining in her routine. Nadia then climbed up a fourth time and completed her dismount.

Nadia received a low score of 7.25, leaving her personally in thirteenth place. Fortunately this score was enough for her hometown team barely to edge out the city of Oradea for the Romanian Junior Gymnastics gold medal. Back in the locker room, Marta Karolyi yelled at Nadia for not concentrating. Bela, however, decided that the best course of action was to treat Nadia kindly and hope that she had learned from the experience. He even went out and bought a special Eskimo doll for her, to make her feel better.

Ten years later, when writing her autobiography, Nadia recalled how the experience of falling off the apparatus three times had inspired her to try harder:

> On the night of our return [from the competition] I sat alone in my room and brooded. I told myself that I was never going to be humiliated in such a way again, and that in future I would take my sport very seriously. I realized that I felt jealous of the winner, that I wanted so badly to trade places with her, and I knew that if I applied myself more fully to my training, I would find that first place very soon. I believed in my own ability and had great faith in my coaches, especially Bela.

From then on, Nadia slept with the Eskimo doll and carried it with her everywhere so that she would always remember to concentrate. Improved concentration helped Nadia come in first in this same tournament the following year, when she was nine. After that first-place finish, Nadia improved so rapidly that even Bela and Marta Karolyi were surprised.

When she was still nine, Nadia was named to the Romanian Girls' Gymnastic Team, which meant that she would now travel to other countries to compete. In her first foreign meet, Nadia took first place in the All-Around Competition in Poland. Soon after that, Nadia won gold medals at the 1971 Friendship Cup in Sofia, Bulgaria, in both the uneven parallel bars and the balance beam events.

During the next several years Nadia regularly brought home gold medals and trophies to her family in Oneşti and became well known in her country. When she won three gold medals at the 1973 Friendship Cup in East Germany while competing against Russia's Nelli Kim and other famous gymnasts, Nadia's coaches began to talk about her playing a big role on the 1976 Romanian Olympic Team.

In 1975 Nadia vaulted into the spotlight of the gymnastics world. When she won the Women Champions' Tournament in London in April, newspapers dubbed her a "wonder child." Then in May the thirteen-year-old Nadia became an international gymnastics star of the first magnitude when she won four gold medals and a silver against some of the world's best female gymnasts in the European Championships at Skien, Norway. This performance helped Nadia get voted 1975 Sportswoman of the Year by both European and American sportswriters.

Nadia was pleased when she was named to the Romanian Olympic Team and Bela was named team coach. During that year before the 1976 Olympics, Bela took the girls to as many meets as he could, and Nadia earned one gold medal after another. Finally the event for which Nadia had been training for eight years — the Olympic Games — was held in Montreal, Canada, in July 1976.

Because the Olympics come just once every four years and are considered by many to be the greatest of all sporting events, most athletes are nervous when they perform at the Games. Nadia, however, wasn't fazed at all. By this time she had done many of her routines so many thousands of times that they seemed easy to her.

On Sunday, July 18, eighteen thousand people in the Forum at Montreal watched as the gymnasts took the floor to perform the Compulsory Exercises — events all the gymnasts are required to do. Although gymnasts from various countries performed simultaneously, nearly everyone's eyes were focused on Nadia as she leaped and twirled and did handsprings and somersaults on the equipment. She was so graceful, strong, and well coordinated that when she swung round and round the uneven parallel bars there were moments when it seemed as if she were about to defy gravity and not come back down to earth!

In the Olympics, four judges vote on the performance of each gymnast, with the score determined by discarding the highest and lowest figures and averaging the two middle scores. The top score that can be attained is 10.0. The scoring was high on that Sunday night, with many of the athletes reaching high in the nines. As Nadia dismounted from the uneven parallel bars, people in the audience wondered if she would receive 9.7 or even 9.8. But then a strange thing occurred: the scoreboard lit up with a 1.00.

For a moment, the audience sat puzzled. Then there was an explosive burst of applause as people realized what had happened. The judges had awarded Nadia a perfect 10.0, but the electronic scoreboard, which was programmed to go only up to 9.99, couldn't record her score. The four-foot-eleven-inch, eighty-six-pound fourteen-year-old girl had become the first gymnast in the modern Olympic Games to achieve a perfect score!

One might have to look back to the ancient Olympic Games, when great champions were treated almost like gods, to match the kind of praise Nadia received on that Sunday night and during the next few days. Nadia — who ultimately earned a total of seven perfect scores and won three gold medals during the 1976 Olympics — was called "Little Miss Perfect" and "The Princess of the Games" by TV announcers and journalists. Her coach, Bela Karolyi, said, "Nadia is the best gymnast in the world." Some experts called her the greatest gymnast who had ever lived!

Nadia seemed happier that her team had won the silver (second-place) medal for all-round team gymnastics than she was about her own amazing accomplishments. Again and again the serious girl with the large brown eyes was asked how she could be so calm about her feats. Clutching her Eskimo doll, she told them, "I worked very hard, very seriously. I knew I would win!" Then, perhaps because she thought she sounded conceited, she smiled and added, "But I want to keep improving!"

Although it was nearly impossible for Nadia ever again to match her 1976 Olympic performance, she did continue to do very well. In the 1980 Olympic Games in Moscow, when she was eighteen years old, Nadia won two gold medals and an overall silver medal. Still, Nadia Comaneci, who later trained other gymnasts and served as a judge of gymnastic events, will always be remembered for her perfect scores in the 1976 Olympics.

Tracy Austin

(born in 1962)

Two-and-a-half-year-old Tracy Austin picked up
the tennis racket and ball that someone had left in
the living room and began playing with them. She
held the tennis racket as tightly as she could, tossed
the ball up, and swung. BAM! She struck a lamp
with the racket and down it went. Tracy picked up
the ball and swung at it again several times, knocking over other small pieces of furniture in the process.

Fortunately, several members of the family
heard the noise and rushed to Tracy before she
could destroy the entire living room. As she sur-
veyed the damage, Mrs. Austin said that they had

better take Tracy out to the tennis courts before she wrecked the house.

Tracy Austin was the baby of a family of tennis players. Her parents, Jeanne and George Austin, had been playing the game for years at the courts near their home in Rolling Hills, California. Tracy's older sister and three older brothers often brought home tennis trophies for their outstanding play. Soon after the incident in the living room, Tracy's family took her out to the tennis courts, but there was one big problem. The racket was almost as tall as Tracy! Mr. Austin, a nuclear physicist for an aerospace company, solved this problem by sawing the end off a racket for his youngest child.

At first Tracy was content to hit the ball off the backboard while her parents, her sister, Pam, and her brothers, Jeff, Doug, and John, played games. But hitting the ball off the backboard came so easily to Tracy that soon she was pestering everyone in her family to play games with her. Although Tracy couldn't see over the net, her family was amazed at the way the three-year-old slammed the ball. So serious was Tracy about the game that her parents enrolled her in a class for little children run by Vic Braden, a well-known tennis teacher in Rolling Hills.

By the age of four, Tracy was spending much of her time at the tennis courts. When she wasn't taking lessons from Coach Braden, she would play anyone who would take her on. Tracy was so in love with tennis that people worried about her lack of interest in other things. "We tried to get her to play with dolls," Vic Braden said later, after Tracy had become a famous tennis player. "But she'd say no — she just wanted to hit the tennis ball."

Even when Tracy was just four and five years old, people in the tennis world began to take note of her. In July 1967 her picture appeared on the cover of *World Tennis* magazine, with a caption saying: "Tracy Austin, Age 4, Has Been Playing Tennis for Two Years." Tracy was five when Billie Jean King, one of the best female tennis players of all time, stopped at the club in Rolling Hills and watched her play for a while. "That kid's going to be great!" King predicted, as Tracy slammed the ball.

By the time she was in first grade, Tracy was regularly competing against college students and adults and was developing her own personal style. She liked to hit her backhand with both hands to increase her power, and she loved to charge the net and hit the ball on the fly. Although her brothers and sister and most other older players could easily beat her, Tracy learned a great deal about various tennis strokes and about competition while playing them. There was another advantage to playing older people. Competing against people her own age seemed easy by comparison!

About the time of Tracy's seventh birthday,

her family and Coach Braden decided that she was ready for tournament play. In her first tournament, Tracy lost to a girl nearly twice her age, but after that she began to win nearly every tournament she entered. When she was still seven, she won the Los Angeles Metropolitan City Championship for girls ten and under. At nine she won the nationwide championship for girls twelve and under and also decided upon a major goal in life. She was watching a match between Chris Evert and Evonne Goolagong on television when suddenly she turned to her mother and said: "I'm going to be the best tennis player in the world someday!"

At eleven and at twelve, Tracy played in numerous junior tournaments around the country and brought home trophies and awards at an amazing rate. Experts called her a "tennis prodigy" and even a "genius." When reporters asked her how she had become so good at such an early age, Tracy would respond: "I started when I was so young," or "Tennis is the family sport." Since she had been good at tennis for as long as she could remember, it didn't occur to her to be conceited about her accomplishments.

Tracy was about thirteen when she realized that she was going to have to live two separate lives. On the one hand, she was what she often referred to as a "normal kid." With her blonde pigtails and braces on her teeth, she looked much like dozens of other girls at the Dapple Gray Intermediate School. She did all the things that the other girls did, too — collecting stickers to put in her notebooks, stopping at the store after school to buy snacks, sometimes putting off her homework until the last minute.

In one big way, however, Tracy was different from every other girl at her school. She was one of the most talented, dedicated, and competitive young tennis players in the world. Tracy kept her tennis personality so distinct from her young-girl self that people who saw her play for the first time were often stunned. They found it difficult to believe that the girl with the pigtails, sweet smile, and braces could become so ferocious on the tennis court.

When Tracy Austin was thirteen and fourteen, people began to wonder how she would do against top-ranked adults. Tracy, who was wondering that herself, heard that a professional women's tournament was scheduled for early 1977 in Portland, Oregon. Her brother Jeff would be playing in a men's pro tournament there at the same time. Mr. and Mrs. Austin allowed Tracy to enter the tournament, and in January 1977 she accompanied her twenty-five-year-old brother to Oregon.

When reporters learned that Tracy was playing in the Avon Futures Tournament, they asked her if she thought she had a chance to win. "I'm just going there for the practice," she answered.

But when the tournament began, Tracy beat one seasoned tennis player after the other. When she defeated a California star, Stacy Margolin, in the finals, it meant that fourteen-year-old Tracy had won a professional tournament. Had she been a professional herself, Tracy would have received several thousand dollars for this triumph. But because she was an amateur, Tracy had to settle for the honor of having beaten a group of outstanding women players.

The Avon Futures victory was the start of a wonderful year for Tracy. One spring day when she arrived home from school, she found a letter from London awaiting her. Tracy opened the envelope and discovered that she had been invited to Wimbledon to play in the most famous tennis tournament in the world — the All-England Championships. Tracy, who had just become the youngest player ever invited to play in this great tournament, dashed into the kitchen, shouting, "Mom, guess what? I'm invited to play at *Wimbledon!*"

Tracy arrived in England with her family on a cold, rainy summer day in 1977. Once she reached Wimbledon, Tracy was a little awed by the traditions and great players. When she saw Jimmy Connors, Chris Evert, Arthur Ashe, and other famous tennis players walking around, her first impulse was to ask them for their autographs.

Tracy's first Wimbledon opponent was Elly

Vessies-Appel of the Netherlands. In tennis, the first player to win at least six games and be at least two games ahead is the winner of a *set*. In women's tennis, the first player to win two sets wins the *match*. With her mother, father, sister, and grandmother watching, Tracy won her match with Elly Vessies-Appel by a score of 6–3, 6–3.

After that first-round victory, the tennis world went berserk over the fourteen-year-old girl in pigtails and braces. On the sports pages of newspapers worldwide, Tracy was called "Little Miss Marvel," "Shirley Temple in Tennis Shoes," "The Pigtail Princess," and "The Mighty Muppet."

For her next opponent, Tracy drew Chris Evert, who had been the number one female tennis player in the world for the preceding four years. If Tracy could beat Chris, it would be the equivalent of a fourteen-year-old pitcher's defeating the New York Yankees or a fourteen-year-old basketball player's beating an NBA all-star one-on-one. Eighteen thousand people crowded around Wimbledon's famed Centre Court to see if Tracy could do it.

For a short while, it appeared that Tracy might. The recent junior-high-school graduate hit several powerful deep shots and took the first game. Most of the spectators were cheering for Tracy, and this seemed to upset Chris Evert a bit. Nonetheless Chris, who was eight years older than Tracy, began slamming deep shots of her own and was soon beating the young Californian in game after game. In the end, Chris Evert took the match by a score of 6–1, 6–1. Although Tracy would much rather have won, she was pleased to have battled Chris so hard. She knew that if she kept playing hard and practicing, she would probably get a chance to play Chris Evert again.

Several months later, in September 1977, Tracy went to Forest Hills, New York, to compete in her home country's most important tournament — the U.S. Open Championship. While her classmates were beginning high school, Tracy was competing against some of the world's best tennis stars. Amazingly, Tracy began the tournament by beating four top stars in a row. Although the outstanding Betty Stove of the Netherlands then knocked her out of the tournament, Tracy had proved herself a powerful force in the tennis world.

Tracy was now faced with a decision — whether or not to turn professional. If she did, she could earn as much as half a million dollars a year in prize money. On the other hand, turning pro would mean she wouldn't be eligible for the amateur tournaments she loved to play in. More important, the pressure to win money might cause her to "burn out" at an early age, as has happened to many young athletes in various sports. Although Tracy decided to retain her amateur status for a while, she did so well against the world's top tennis stars in 1978 that she finally turned pro in October of that year.

In her first pro tournament in Stuttgart, West Germany, Tracy's first-place finish earned her six thousand dollars and a new red Porsche. During her first year as a pro Tracy earned more than three hundred thousand dollars as she won tournaments in such places as Hilton Head, South Carolina, and Rome.

Tracy's life as a tennis pro was not as glamorous as you might think. She had to travel a great deal, practice at least three hours a day, run regularly to stay in condition, and be careful about her diet to maintain her good health. What made things doubly difficult for Tracy was the fact that she was still a high-school student. She took her schoolwork with her to the tournaments. While the other players were off relaxing at a restaurant or a disco, Tracy was often in her hotel room studying American history or English composition under her mother's supervision. Despite having to do her schoolwork at odd times, Tracy managed to maintain nearly a straight-A average.

One tournament that Tracy was especially looking forward to was the U.S. Open in September of 1979. Tracy played so well at the beginning of the tournament that there was very little drama. After mowing down one opponent after another she found herself facing the great Chris Evert once again, this time for the championship.

Tracy had greatly improved since her loss to Evert at Wimbledon in 1977, yet few people gave her much of a chance against Chris, who had won the U.S. Open four straight times. Even after Tracy won the first set, 6–4, thousands of people watching the match in person and millions more watching on TV figured that Chris would come roaring back and win the next two sets to retain her title.

Tracy Austin continued to outvolley, outmaneuver, and even outthink Chris Evert, however, and finally the stunned viewers realized that Tracy was about to do it. She was ahead in the second set, 5–3, and needed just one more point to win the game, set, and championship.

As Tracy was about to serve, someone in the crowd called "Let's go, Tracy!" and someone else yelled "C'mon, Tracy!" Tracy Austin served, and when Chris Evert hit the ball into the net a few seconds later, the match was over. Sixteen-year-old Tracy Austin had become the youngest player — female or male — ever to win the U.S. Open Championship.

Tracy Austin followed her 1979 championship with many more victories, and by the age of eighteen she had earned well over a million dollars in prize money. Unfortunately, Tracy injured her back

in early 1981, but she worked with her usual determination to regain her strength, and later that same year she won the U.S. Open for the second time. By the age of twenty she had earned a reputation as one of the greatest players in the history of women's tennis.